THE BEST AUSTRALIAN
POEMS
20
13

THE BEST AUSTRALIAN
POEMS

EDITED BY LISA GORTON

Black Inc.

Published by Black Inc.,
an imprint of Schwartz Media Pty Ltd
37–39 Langridge Street
Collingwood VIC 3066 Australia
email: enquiries@blackincbooks.com
http://www.blackincbooks.com

ISBN 9781863956277

Printed in Australia by Griffin Press. The paper this book is printed on
is certified against the Forest Stewardship Council® Standards.
Griffin Press holds FSC chain of custody certification SGS-COC-005088.
FSC promotes environmentally responsible, socially beneficial
and economically viable management of the world's forests.

Contents

Introduction

IN THIS ANTHOLOGY THE POEMS ARE SET OUT ALPHBET-
ically because I have selected poems, not poets. Many of the
poets whose work I like best do not have poems in this book,
perhaps through an accident of timing or because their poems
work not singly but in collections. More, though, the poems are
set out alphabetically to bring home the ritual and music of
language, always more at play in poetry than in prose.

The anthology is an abcedarium. Its poems set off through the
letters of the alphabet – the first signs, the fixed sounds, so
habitual to thought they can seem real, which are invented. In
1894 Mallarmé declared, 'Speech is no more than a commercial
approach to reality.' One way or another, poetry's play of language
works to restore that relationship between speech and reality – or,
at least, between speech and experience.

An anthology is essentially arbitrary – especially one such as
this, composed of individual poems. Beyond the vagaries of selec-
tion, even its structure is arbitrary. Open it anywhere and you
find yourself at a beginning. If the structure of any book makes a
not-to-scale model of time, this anthology offers an experience of
time that is now, and now, and now – instants that replace each
other. It has no chronology and no main line; a reader can move
through it in any direction at will. I hope the experience of
reading this anthology will bring into question how far those
abstractions – 'best', 'Australian', '2013' – exist in fact, and what
end they serve as one thinks about the poems collected here.

What characterises Australian poetry now is its variousness: a
play of forms and registers and voices, not only from poem to poem

but within poems, too. Here are collage poems with a confessional impulse, short short stories, late surrealist couplets, poems that weave satire and lyric together, fragmentary essays in epistles, metaphysical pastorals, epic narratives glimpsed through keyhole lyrics, and lyrics that explode the idea of what a lyric can say, and be.

This variousness – hybridity, flexibility – suggests a new concept of influence, far from the 'anxiety of influence' that Harold Bloom defined forty years ago. Though Bloom's idea of some binary opposition between tradition and the avant-garde persists in some poetry criticism, it hardly helps to understand the free play of influence in Australian poetry now.

Maybe that sense of free play comes from a different version of poetic tradition, one the Net has made possible: poetic tradition outside institutional control, revealed not as a monolith but as a history of reading, as wayward and curious as reading is. Any Ern Malley, dreamt up now, would have read poetry from around the world and across history, a tradition at once instantaneous and disorderly.

A poetic tradition, though it might seem authoritative ('best', 'Australian', '2013'), is a chancy and contradictory thing, a clustering web of connections between writers, which, because influence works so oddly, has many nodes and outposts, threads that stretch across borders of nation and language. The Net can serve as an image of this version of tradition, in which one poem opens into another poem, and another, and again. The mind, through the screen, takes possession of prosthetic memory; proliferation and deferral make up its experience of time, and together conceal its many blind spots, limits and distortions. Beyond anxieties about the economics of bookselling and the printed word, this version of tradition seems to me the most intriguing consequence of new technology. Some recent instances of plagiarism are disturbing most of all because they corrupt these experiences of discovery.

It is no paradox that poetry on the Net – endless, unfolding, indefinite – brings home the importance of local places and printed books, which, exactly because they are singular and confined, can pass into history and become the holding place of memories and arguments. Poetry, whose forms close in time, is a kind of writing that justifies the printed book – an artefact. As commercial interests overrun the Net, the privacy of a printed book shows again its value. Libraries are burying their books too soon.

It seems to me that poetry, more quickly than prose, has registered these changes: this free play of influence, and the question of what survives, what goes beyond parody. In the several thousand poems that I read for this anthology, I looked for ones that seemed to me surprising, generative, memorable. If the making of a poem is a series of decisions, transactions with possibility, some poems seem to hold like an electric charge the trace of all those forfeited possibilities.

Various, adaptive, inventive: poetry is everywhere, inventing its own communities, where you can seek it out – in online and paper magazines, newspapers, public readings, performances, reading groups and independent publishing houses. I am grateful to the editors and curators who have allowed Black Inc. to republish poems, and I thank Black Inc. and all the editors who have helped with this anthology, Chris Feik, Kate Goldsworthy, Nikola Lusk and Julian Welch, not only for their calm efficiency but also for their commitment to Australian poetry.

Lisa Gorton

A Denizen

The octopus is dead
who lived in Wylies Baths
below the circus balustrade
and the chocked sea tiles.

Old legerdemain of eight
died of too much chlorine
applied to purify the amenities
of urine and algal slippage.

Favourite of chivvying children
the one who could conform
its elastics with any current
or hang from its cupped feet

now lies, slop biltong
beak and extinct pasta
out in the throwaway tide
and will leave with the wobbegong.

Les Murray

A Dire Season

from Devadatta's Poems

A star had appeared in the night sky,
it was long and pointed as an adder's tooth.
The moon rose putrescent, bloody. All our
elephants had turned viridian-eyed, wild.
Dozens of snakes hissed as though a fierce
wind blew. Many children fell ill,

tottered on legs like blown-up bladders.
All we could do was summon the Brahmins,
watch as they poured ghee over the altars
and burnt our cattle in sacrifice. After a week
we had little left to offer, though we still
dug fields, hauled water, turned the loam.

We all felt Kapilavatthu was done for,
that not one of those Brahmins had the verses
to save us. We drank bitter herbs,
flailed our skin with twigs we bought
from the broom makers, cut our arms
with shards from the potters' workshops.

We fingered crimson beads and performed
small dry ceremonies in the dirt. Before
that season finally turned, I'd often long
for Siddhattha, for the little tunes he could play
on his thin, twisted stems of grass.
Something about his notes, their fine weaving

through the dusk. When I listened, I thought
of our clay daub, mud brick and whitewashed
town as a grand place, one whose streets
you could walk down squaring your shoulders,
knowing that the gods supped at the flames
that burnt on our altars. I don't know

what Siddhattha heard in the notes.
Perhaps he foresaw the rise of the rivers,
border conflicts in the west, heard the screams
of our women and children, saw the smoke
and the fires, saw Kapilavatthu overrun
with Brahmins carrying slaughtered oxen

and antelope aloft from all our fire hearths—
all that blood and dung,
all the vulture feathers in their topknots.

Judith Beveridge

A disaster

Here, too, some ground has been cleared
by the square of its distance. He wasn't specific,
but more or less conceded he had elaborated the mad
scheme that first gripped him as a student, the day he
sat down together on the sofa, fifty yards of absolute
darkness pocketing interjections as the years passed
and the stunlight flickered. He turned to Dalgliesh,
I mean Newton, and said: "What's the matter?
What did she say?" No one answered, but the
crowd edged forward expectantly, having paid
in good faith for an admission. He said Grace
had the task of feeding the hens the details of her
physical presence, and that his own individual cells
had challenged the quantum flux to a duck race:
having found a way to go wayward faster,
he'd lost to his lucky stars — a disaster!

('A disaster' borrows words and phrases from Timothy Ferris's Coming
of Age in the Milky Way and from P.D. James's A Dalgliesh
Trilogy.)

Chris Edwards

A quick drink at the bar

Nothing mystical, it's like 'hey have an aspirin'
  the crazy breeders uttering injunctions like painted blue jays.
   When they get to town nobody sleeps until they're gone

willy-nilly as divine accidents amid the particularity of things.
  Inert as an absurdly large rule, they are
   nothing mystical, like 'hey have a complex insecurity'

categorical with basic speech, this awkward climate
  of hierarchies confused with delight.
   When they get to town nobody sleeps until they're gone

and nobody enters the *yes-no* dualism of *I-don't-know* ... underfoot
  the ground trickles with cats, trees, history
   it's nothing mystical, it's like 'hey have a programmatic soul'

they're smiling back like boring paintings or a hands-on cure
  rehearsing with ginger ale.
   When they get to town nobody sleeps until they're gone

casual as cut moonlight
  and lonely as a surgical experience, pleasantly moist;
   nothing mystical, it's like 'hey have an aspirin'
   when they get to town nobody sleeps until they're gone.

Dan Disney

An Ordinary Evening in Newtown

1

Camperdown's for dogs,
Friday evening in the park off Church Street

a barefoot man
carries a plank:
                          it's like
La Grande Jatte
for Airedales
                     under the flight path

2

a square-faced guy
underpants protruding from his jeans
in the smoky atmosphere of the Court House

the word HOT, above the wood roof of the outside bar
(neon in daylight)

'are you fuckin married or what!?'

3

in the Carlisle Castle 'Crimson & Clover',
the forty-somethings

(Church T-shirt,
dingo before pyramid)

vivid pink drinks,
a faint vomit smell from the kitchen (cheese?)

and now, the meat raffle
'looks nice, but I've nowhere to cook it'

Laurie Duggan

And Then a Cup of Tea

The Captain had a kipper from a previous daring breakfast
Lodged dangerously close to his spine;
But still he led his men.
When he stepped from the wooden dinghy and waded ashore
He was picking his teeth bravely with a fish-bone.
The sun rose behind him and broke its yolk upon the New World;
It flowed golden.
Grinning, he dipped his little soldiers in it.

Mal McKimmie

Another Chardin in Need of Cleaning

after Frank O'Hara

Forearmed is foredefeated,
a spragged illusion that had me forever
check the silver-leafed backing.
What seemed like a vermillion mirror of sea,
the work of rash gods competing over
nose-powder and light. Salient image
as tonnage of froth, the superficial pleasure
of being someone else for the day.
What wasn't there cannot disappear,
so why regret that awkward kiss
over the smoker's box
when you decided to sit and clean the turnips.
One employs colours in the afternoon glare
but my feelings remain diffuse.
Each memory from the same genre,
duly sentimental,
yet indistinguishable in the over-populated world.
Does it matter who can gauge the lapping dark
for you were everything once
returning to dead layer, a general of still life
hanging on the end of the dauphine's stays.

Ann Vickery

As Flames Were My Only Witness

After three days of wind pounding the midriff of hills
and nights of dry lightning fracturing the sky
into the crazing of old porcelain it was no surprise
when it came. In five minutes a towering cauliflower

was spilling white curds, froth and tumultuous blossom,
a fractal coolly replicating from a moment
that was now far below, with birds
like flakes of soot tossed in its turbulence,
their cries plangent and scattering, and consumed.

Driving beneath into that apricot-soft light
was like being inside an evangelist's blimp:
a dome of chapel stillness, except for little flames
at the hem like small faces sneaking entry under.

For a moment there was a benign peace
as is said of those hazy, uncertain states:
the womb, anaesthesia, drowning.

We think we know silence, it is our blue Pacific:
the refrigerated, drained, arrhythmical kind,
and the cupped, hill-to-hill kind, with a dog's bark
or the crack of a breaking branch to give it scale.

This was something else—dense and pressing,
even in that beguiling peace,
vast and lonely as the space that clears
the moment before judgement.

Russell Erwin

As in the future when

a big computer was doing the thinking
for us, but fortunately feelings
proved stronger in the end

I was feeling little except for a soggy film
brochure containing a childhood story
a forgotten dictator getting dug up and researched
still a hero to some

the light from the window lit everything a
special poetic shade of red
                         Snow
on the mountains behind the apartment buildings
giving the former solidity if not—

but I am carrying on
collecting the action figures before
the film's even started

a desire to be obsolete, to retire
to one's ancestral seat
or to have your computer write
your poem for you: these are the same

yet the mountains do return
some unassuming zest to the painting, suggestive
of low-linteled houses on the other side with plots
sprouting flash frozen veg, still green,
that will soon turn round and return the suggestion

Jal Nicholl

At Lerici

for Carlo Olivieri

Darkly at anchor
in the roadstead, ships keep close
the secret of their journeys,
and the islands theirs.

History is made up
of nights such as this when little happens.

Lovers in their beds
whisper and touch, a new player
tumbles onto the scene.
Crickets strike up
a riff on the razzle-dazzle
of starlight, then stop.

The blissful friction and pointillist
throb of night music
is older, runs deeper
than speech. An electric
flicker the planet's first

incidence of traffic.
Then heartbeat. Then thought.

We sit in the warm dark watching
container-ships ride
on blue-black moonlit glitters.

After long
journeying arrived at the high tide
of silence, after talk.

David Malouf

Autoethnographic

And still the feeling hadn't left us, something had
been missing all the while, back there, beyond
the Great Forgetting. Worse, the moments when
we could convince each other it wasn't not there
had become fewer and further between, a daily
clutch of episodes before that great ocean of
mind would slink in, cruelling. It was a junkyard,
a shipwreck, a six car pile-up at the end of our
tongues, perfectly out of reach. Georgia suggested
we were characters in a pilot for a TV series that
never went to air. Someone had been picking
us off one-by-one since the last ad break, taking
the weakest, the meanderer at the back of the
pack, the sweaty little accountant with the pocket-
protector and broken glasses, the cheerleader in
matching Adidas skirt and mules. There had been
a series of pits, balled spikes, bear traps, bodiless
hands reaching from the brush, faces concealed
in sweat-stained hoodies looming out of the
damp forest that was otherwise so distractingly
scenic and exploitable. At night we could hear the
muffled breathing nearby, a hunter's soft treat,
voices turned low plotting in a language all their
own. We were in a forest of cannibals, overrun
by human sacrifice, suicide bombers, terrorists,
sub-prime mortgages and hoodlum cross-dressing
freaks. Each morning we took a head count
and the two of us were still there, while the day
stretched on repetitive and overfull with promise.
The coast was just beyond the next rise, we would
meet the friendly locals who would offer us the
choice bits of their exotic cuisine and ancient folk

wisdom, then validate our parking tickets before guiding us to the safety of a shopping mall. But Georgia was adamant, it was a cliffhanger we would never get to the end of. We were stranded, facing each other with only our fear.

Michael Brennan

Basic Hut Methodology

take your platform boots off
Kevin
    you've killed a deer to make your point
but our tea and biscuit sensibilities
will cope
we forgive you
    you're charming!
hiding from your vanity
             likening molten glass to tartiflette

in the fresh peat you hammer a sign
'Not Hobbit-Town' (it's cute)
then later tell the production crew (sternly)
"this not aspirational! This is economical!"

Marxism 101 plaything
soliloquies about the means of production
          while you go on dung safari

afterwards the gang pretends to piss in a bucket
you call the result a "manly amount"

150 years of Britain's industrial history
at the bottom of a Hackney canal
which swallows your magnet with an erotic slurp

there you go all doe-eyed
banging on the shed roof
but we're weary
       of plumbing double entendre

Kevin and the engineer boil a kettle

"shall I play mother?"

that curve came from a tree
    gun powder tamped into the trunk
    a certain "massive quality"

boy with a simple dream
to own a patch of woodland
(where there's a thing there's a fence)

your friends show how they feel
by building a a straw effigy
    and lighting it with flaming arrows

Ella O'Keefe

Black Throated Finch

By the pool, their fingernail-sized gullets undulate briskly
As if they are guilty celebrities scoffing a midnight treat,
Their black cravats panting with excitement. They can't
Stay in this kitchen heat for long; fluent in the language
Of dehydration, a fast tipple or else they're dumbstruck.
Their image burned into extinction's cyclopean retina,
As if this fragile flock gazed into the sun directly, or they
Were a picnic of ants fried by a bully's magnifying glass.
The dam water is a current running through their bodies;
It sets off the electricity of their flight, as one they scatter
To the air, like a handful of wedding rice. Their fall might
Weigh as much; in the billionaire's thoughts he's ripped
Out the earth's coal-black throat; the box trees cut open
Like rich sediment. Their habitat halved like a seed cake.

Brett Dionysius

Blind Spot

Slip id to lop its
nob, lost din on lip's nil boil,
dot sin's lid to sop.

Slits' slop spills to list lost. Slip
lip blot to top, lob it up,

spin bits to bile, so
pot nibs to soil n sob n
lop it lop its top.

Justin Clemens

Bringing You Home

You've stained my sleep again and your tiny clothes
tangle their arms and legs in my washing machine.
So many headless bodies
and now your wriggly purple flesh,
two white straps on a new white nappy, wet,
wet, wet, urine soaks it, and you, and me,
before I can hook your spider legs
back into their flowered net.
Dark silk clings to your skinny neck,
yet no spider ever lifted sounds like this.
Your eyes are marbles in a slow slot-machine
and there you've scratched your face again.
It's time to snare those starfish hands—
but God, how to blunt such silver flecks?

Susan Fealy

Bushfire Approaching

I

I am ready to evacuate if need be.
My wife emailed to say a fire is out of control
on Julimar Road, less than ten kilometres away.
She says she'll return with the car, but I say it's okay,
we'll monitor and speak through the gaps.
She insists she will return: listening to the chat
in the library at Toodyay, seeing smoke in the west,
checking the FESA site. I say I will take a look outside
and get back to her in minutes. She is waiting. I climb
the block gingerly with my torn calf muscle striking back,
and see the growing pall over Julimar. A great firebreak
and a bitumen road are between here and there, I reassure,
though I will keep a close eye on it. The breeze blows
from the east, but is ambivalent and could swing
about. There are no semantics in this. And Paul Auster
is right where William (the lumberman) Bronk was wrong:
the poem doesn't happen in words, but 'between seeing
the thing and making it into a word'. *Location location location.*
As evidence: if fire sweeps through, only the mangled
metal of this Hermes typewriter will remain,
a witness, philosophy in-situ vanquished, and an elegy
made from bits of a different seeing with different words,
remain. Figurative density will take hold, and landscape
will be less fragile, the font more robust. It won't rely
on paper: ash become an idea, a taste for some.
You stop seeing the red when it's on top of you.
But true burning feeds on ash and the idea
of fire: it perseveres and requires only oxygen
and memory. Wild oats caught in my socks
taunt my ankles. Fuel for fire. In all seriousness.

II

I am not hearing AC/DC's 'This House is on Fire'
out of perversity. This morning a rush of colour
brought on a flashback, and I've not had one of those
for a decade. Strychnine-saturated, like the bush
where rangers claim to conserve native species
through poisoned baits. Rapid heartbeat, dry mouth,
outbreaks of laughter (grotesque, face of death),
colour codings of annihilation: spiritual and topographical.
Phantasm of acid trips – pink batts, supermen, green dragons,
orange barrels, purple hearts, clearlights, ceramic squares,
goldflakes, microdots, lightning bolts: nomenclature
of William Blake and weird melancholy of habitat loss.
Lost and unfounded. A run on images. Voices in the room.
Excruciating paranoid cartoon violence. So, I check
outside again and the plume is still moving southwest
though the wind is tentative and temperature
up five degrees over the last thirty minutes. This is realtime,
unlike hypnogogia, hallucinations? Grounds for worship.
Foundational ontology. I should mention that I have flu
and that's why I stayed home in the first place. Harvest
is full-on though I have finished grass cutting here.
I wore myself out and my defences are down. Run down.
Antibodies hesitant if not docile. I make rhetoric
out of the flood of image-fragments: seems like good sense,
making the best, keeping a grip, cool in a volatile situation?

III

I'm abandoning my poem on the wheatbelt stone gecko
and the 'keeled tail' of a black-headed monitor
which is running amok through the roof, along walls,
scaling trees with maritime skill. The images lack
explanation and coalesce, are minimalist, but will
serve as a poor kind of last will and testament.
One sheet in my pocket, and it will be this.

IV

The wind has dropped, though smoke – not impenetrable
but more substantial than 'thin' – hangs over the block,
a tentative fallout. The birds are doing their silence
thing, or have shot through. We keep no birds in coops.
The air is almost acrid. Defend or abandon?
It's when the smell of burning reaches upwind
that you know it has bitten deep. Firebreaks: check.
Water: check, but if the pump goes that's an end to flow.
Fireblanket: check. Personal papers and evacuation pack: check.
No room for 'literature': just this poem, paperweight.
Ready to lend a helping hand: always, to best of ability.
Essential medications. Maybe the boy's most precious toy,
but he wouldn't expect it. Something of my wife's.
Insects thick on the flyscreens: suddenly Hitchcockian.

V

Smoke-mushrooms are haloes about wattles they haven't yet touched
where it counts. Prelude. Early life of devastation, its long legacy
too long in its brief moment of, well, beauty. Back again after
staggering uphill – glimpses of lush green moss amidst stubble
and granite are bemusing and bizarrely cheering – and all is suddenly
military, warzone, combat. Helitacs, fixed-winged water bombers
coming over the hills. Dousing. Or maybe it's anti-militaristic?
No time to think about this. Three years ago, fire destroyed
forty homes just south of here. It was like this then, too.

VI

Alert Level: 'a bushfire is burning near Julimar and Kane Roads';
'stay alert and monitor your surroundings'; why use quote marks?
This is barely copyright in the life and death of it. Plagiarism?
Blame burns with a heat unlike any other and burns long
after last embers have faded. And with days of heat and high
winds ahead, even a dead ember might find heart again, and leap
to the occasion. Elemental showdown. Proof. Precedent.

Test case. Habeas corpus – the body present. The burning
question: people build houses in the bush, then blame the bush.
My brother, life-long surfer, says: If I get taken by a shark
remember it was while doing something I love in its universe.
Remember me in this light. The fire has jumped Julimar Road.

John Kinsella

Chimney

By day it does its thick and heinous work,
    only slowly,
clogged with the sweat
    of coal, meat, sticks and wood.
It is like a character from folklore
    —or something older—transmogrified
into this domestic hunkering
    of brick and soot.

          *

In the evening it partakes, ominously,
    of the sky's transfiguration into night.
When the men and women have come and gone,
    like loaves of bread,
and the darkness solidifies and the children dream,
    the cold of the planets begins to seep in.
Before dawn, with the embers quiet,
    the chimney opens itself to the stars' dying light

Maria Takolander

from Chinatowns

Over and over you study the menus, the recipes, the difficult names
of herbs and roots, the cures that awaken a forgotten hunger.
You scour these Chinatowns of the mind, translating them
like sutras Xuan Zang fetched from India, testing ways
return might be possible against these homesick inventions,
trace the traveller's alien steps across borders, and in between
discover how transit has a way of lasting, the way these Chinatowns
grew out of not knowing to return or to stay, and then became
    home.

Kim Cheng Boey

City workers during morning rush hour, Collins Street, Melbourne, 2013

Perhaps not fully awake, elbowed and bumped, you alight from trams,
Exit Parliament Station, to join the ballet of the brisk.
Rebel by sitting on a park bench. Such a luxury may incite a
Scowl on a passing face. Reading the
Obituaries in *The Age*, you'll learn how often a certain
Nuclear scientist was married. This knowledge of a more troubled life may
Allow you to take a break from painting the town grey.
Look at the bird borrowed sky. It's not raining rats and tarantulas.

What a gift is hunger. Because of it your ancestors left their caves,
Explored plains, valleys, rivers, seas. These
Adventures became paintings, songs, tall tales, family legends, headlines.
There's the story of each person, on the trains, trams and street corners.
How vulnerable you are, how strong you are. I want to reveal your
Essence via the camera of this poem, as you swarm and
Rush in the business district, glancing at your wristwatches.

Peter Bakowski

Closed on Mondays

too nice
&   when you leave

everything is white noise,
no traffic,
no music,   no muffle,
just thick air
whirring

greyness leaks
into the afternoon,
a dirty kind of day

kids are rolling
down a mound
of irradiated tilth

the world's
assembled curatariat
is queueing unhappily
for their passes
in light drizzle

perdido's
on eastside
& I'm trying ballerina moves
on the fibre mat,
preceding biceps curls
with pitiful
one kilogram weights

a tiny plastic 'T'
   snipped from
      a price tag,
  caught in the mat

is there any
     news from Mars
  that's better
      than here?

       *

latest is
  R.Mutt's a meme

it was when you said
 "say
  'thanks Marcel'"

       *

death's announced
   to
   a quick declivity
    (joke)
of upload, list & link —
scrolling,
    the final ritual

mourners weeping,
   for themselves,
no ghost
 in the crematorium machine

     *

like Georges Perec wrote —
  Nothing is happening, in fact

every single thing's
       a tourist destination
&
   everything's
      available to everyone

taking phone photos
   of the brickworks stacks
from the back seat
      on saturday night

gawking at the mud
   caked on cars
 drifting
    on the flood plain

       *

time experienced
  as a perpetual rush
     to
     the latest in new

o no
     it's Monday
it's closed

& you reveal
   a dour scepticism
      of pop culture
  but
I'd give it
    another chance

following
   my dorky polestar,

relentlessly discursive

*

open the cider

'thanks Marcel'

*

so you want
        to write in a cave
            <u>&</u>
take your source material
            with you?

*

searching all over
        for the house
            where it's quiet
        because
Wallace Stevens
            says it is

*

a vase
        of droopy roses

fine dust
            covering
                a tower
            of expended
                nivea cream jars

*

&
        when I arrive

there's a manuscript,
poems,   new to me,
open for reading

the first pages
        have
    draft numbers—
Draft #1 Draft #2
            —at the top

before anything else
        the rims around
my eyes
        feel tired

the empty room
        purrs its scope

I imagine
  a well-polished
                furniture voice
trying nonchalance,
    the sheets of typing
                    called
    "my stuff "

                *

    it's coming along

                *

stretch out now,
  a woven plastic lounge

muscle & bone grind
    shoulder bone

grind

warm your dead feet
    beneath the baobab tree

        *

thin transparent oil
        slowly leaks
  from the barrel
      of the souvenir pen,
the plastic historical figure
    no longer slides
      along the mini city backdrop,
        he's stuck
at the bottom of the scene

        *

mid april
  &
      the xmas wreath
is still pinned
  to the front door
    of the neighbour
who died
    on boxing day

Pam Brown

Co. Kerry

for Peter Steele

The very smell of the sea beckons –
pungent, redolent of other shores.
    I walk the beach with my forebears.
    They set off and I returned,
        We have found one another out.

The lighthouse at Fenit
looks in all directions at once:
    comings and goings its only concern.
    This is a place of stone.
        This is where the long view obtains.

Limestone conglomerate
holds it all together.
    Beyond the farthest reach of this ocean,
    someone dear is fading fast away.
        He may be gone as I say these words.

His faith is that he has always been the life
that is leaving him, leaving us.
    The sea beckons. The lighthouse is dark.
    Clouds obscure the high hills, the wind is steady.
        This is where we find ourselves.

Paul Kane

Coastline

I walked along the cliff-top at around eleven
one September morning, wondering why the level
of the sea at the horizon
seems always higher than where I am, even though
the waves kept shuddering into spray on rocks far below.

Was it a kind of horizontal vertigo,
or a species of the sublime, a newly released *cogito*,
I think therefore ... I must be a dwarf
standing on the shoulders of other dwarves, each one shorter
than the one before? I filed this thought for

later use and kept walking past clumps of bustling
grass, on a concrete path glittering in bright sunlight,
past a jogger threshing air,
all elbows, knees and sweat, who paused a moment, oinked,
or so it seemed, and jogged on. The morning light coined

a mint of silver on the ocean, golden shivers
of droughty stalks flared from the footpath's fissures
and I was rich for a moment,
richer than the waterfront exclusionary
viewkeepers, the prinked promenaders, even the cemetery.

I passed a clique of tourists gathered at a corner
of the white retaining fence, where locals reckon
the face of the Virgin Mary
appears each day at around eleven, and armed with cameras
and mobile phones they waited with a calm air as

if faith was merely a matter of patience. I prepared
to wait for a while as well, but nothing appeared

to happen, so I strolled on, dissatisfied
as ever. Back then I wanted to be an anagram
of what I should have been: not a Manager

but a flâneur perhaps, or a traveller or taghairm
prophesying in ox-hide by a stream, or migrate
in reverse to my two great-
grandfathers, Musgrave and Quealy, who lived across the
    Shannon
from each other but never knew it, sang their Hosannas

to different Gods and croaked here only eighty miles
and twenty years apart. Would I assimilate
or be assimilated there,
an exile in a land of unfamiliar rain,
a thonged exotic flaw in emerald terrain?

No theme comes from exile except exile, something
no one bothered to tell the ex-pat generation.
Until now, I thought.
I watched some yachts puff south like beeery slobs, all gut
and no behind. A seagull carried on like a galoot

above my head and then the path began declining
into oblongs balkanized by weed-cracks, kindling
memories of jigsaws:
fitting patiently on wet Sundays piece to piece,
sifting through the pile for the opposite

of a promontory of clous: portly swastikas,
running men, whimsies, wheat sacks,
Swedens, Sulawesis, bits
of continent or a cauliflowered florescence, Mandelbrots
ferning into shapes running through my bloodstream.

And then the bigger pieces: the absent shape of you
to which no piece will fit, like emptied rooms
in a house no longer habitable.
Loss ineluctable: there is no cure, no magic zebra
crossing to a lossless world. Aslant in the breeze

I walked the cliff-top walk, totally alone
at the other end of love, on the way from one littoral
to another, balancing an act
in a world out of balance, piecing together words
to confront something, long ago put to the sword.

Level with my eyes a seagull hovered, motionless
into the wind. I passed beer cans in modern middens,
dandelions on the path's port side
while slowly from the north-east, thunderheads of mackerel-
mottled clouds began to coolly spit on the caramel-

coloured cliffs. It's funny how it worms
its way in, love, diasporated like a swarm
of angry bees bearding a heart.
The continents are the oldest divorcees, having drifted
apart for eons. Next to them we've barely tiffed.

But still you reappear, even if only as a pronoun
which has to be emptied out or not pronounced
as it once was: as you.
Almost anyone could be one of them,
the economy of love which we won't fathom.

You can stand for anyone now, there is no end:
the reader of this poem or the one you need
as elementally as air.
And so I kept on walking, finding in a word the future
and the past in ever-repeating series bearing a kind of fruit

into the present. And as I walked, I came to resemble Achilles
racing the tortoise, never overcoming, in the end, a calculus
of ever decreasing lengths.
But I wasn't frustrated — au contraire — I was fascinated:
for love, like every coastline, properly considered, is infinite.

David Musgrave

Country Chinese Restaurants

There's always one in every town
Coonabarabran: Golden Sea Dragon
Dubbo: Fu Lee Way. Maybe your car
Broke down, or you're on the road
With someone who doesn't love
You anymore. Manjimup: Fu Hua
Kangy Angy: New Shanghai. Always
A fish tank in one corner, walls
Panelled with imitation teak, plastic
Scrolls of misted mountains, water
Falls, a lone man fishing. Toowoomba:
Ni Hao; Wangaratta: Koon Way. Vinyl
Booths, nylon lanterns, laminated
Menus flecked with soy, old prices
Rubbed out and handwritten in pen
A teenage girl at the back, hunched
Over homework, harangued
By her mother into waiting on you
Numurkah: Jung Sung Harbour
Gilgandra: Dragon & Phoenix
The chef has fled and the father
Is frying. They're usually empty now
There's take-away. Four-dollar
Cocktails & paper parasols. Maybe
You're on the run – an unpaid hotel bill
Or worse, looking for something you
Never had. Mudgee: Kai Sun, Wagga:
Lum Inn. The wok-steamed weather
& Confucius in a cookie

Mandy Sayer

Crowded Hour

A, Tangerine, lipstick 1962, daring
Hint of flame and wild behaviour,
E, lemon, sour surprise and rave, your
Suspicious self out for a welcome airing
On Fifth Avenue, your midday saviour
A transparent fellow spirit, the caring
Caress of a martini smoothly preparing
Your conscience to accept a second favour –
Bartender's gift of one half-empty bottle –
I, corn silk hair, love at full throttle,
O, blue shadows, delicate gloom
Pricked with traffic lights in the evening air –
U, olive green of underwater hair –
Scuba, the acronym, in the crowded room.

The Consonants

B, brave brown, C, icicle
Pendant, D, dun though pale,
F for faint mauve, fish and bicycle,
G, gothic paint in a green pail
H, an ambulance red and white,
J, lemon rain, K, snakebite,
L, bandage around M for kill,
N, no concrete freeway crush thrill,
P, torrid personals, Q for Quimper,
R, pale reptile, Sun and beach
And T-shirts, V, abrasive screech
Where a red vixen might scamper.
X is just black, Y mottled spoon,
Z pale grey sleeping under the moon.

John Tranter

Dandelion

Skies cross my window with the sound off;
below a sprung herb shudders at life-speed,
rewound; upstairs letters joined in silence
from a man who was involved but hit upon
a delicate code to tell me of his New Year's Eve
at Graubünden, "firework amazing, very long".
In a drawer of old bills keys to rooms

that stay unlocked. Books everywhere, of course;
among them voices raised and heard, never alone,
the ones married to harp and flute. And luck.
Which of the psalms will hear the clouds as
they pass overhead, a stave of wires their nest?
What makes them beautiful? Why do they tear
themselves apart like ageing stars or clocks?

Will Eaves

Darkness Speaks

None of it is true: I am
neither malevolent nor

mystical. You have nothing
to fear; I am the one who makes

things terribly bright and
dramatic when they need to be.

Like when I spill myself a
little at sunset. Night after

night you dream of me. One day
you will wake up properly,

and there I will be, at last.
Your new and endless climate.

Don't look at me; I don't compose
any *kindertotenlieder*.

David McCooey

Dawn

Dawn finds its way into the house
through every recess,
projecting on to walls oblique
slow-motion shadow cinema:
toy canoe and sailing boat
navigate the bathroom wall;
a trompe l'oeil window onto moving trees
configures near a kitchen cabinet;
water, in an unwashed bowl,
attuned to some vibration
ripples across the ceiling;
a teaspoon on a sill glances ...
through cracks and keyholes, light
lets itself into the house,
not as a sly intruder
but with radiant in-pouring,
a casual, brilliant right of entry

Sarah Day

Diary Poem: Uses of Frank O'Hara

Years ago when John Forbes praised
my later work, he said my *Problem
of Evil* was influenced by Tranter's
Red Movie, and being younger and furiouser,
I rang Forbes and explained *P. of E.*
was actually written first. The paper
printed an apology but wicked Forbes
started at once to speculate that Tranter
had based *Red Movie* on *P. of E.*, a claim
of which I thought I'd better warn Tranter,
                          who laughed:
'Anxieties of Influence', and that phrase
came back to me recently when a reviewer
said I'd learned a lot from Frank O'Hara.
I explained to my daughter I'd never
read O'Hara and she, the Fire Tiger,
defended me on those grounds, so the reviewer
professed shock that I had never read O'Hara.
I wondered: am I shocked myself
really that I've never read O'Hara? I do
not miss O'Hara, but I said I would
write a poem called *Frank and I* about us.
The imaginary O'Hara would confess
of course that he has not read me either,
despite which we would feel quite at home.
I see us relaxed on a gritty tenement balcony
on a star-chilled American evening
with drinks in our numb hands speculating
why poetry is so much about denying
what one is not, and why anxiety
about influence is stubbornly so scary.
'I've heard you use long lines', I

would say, and explain, 'The longer
lines in my last book were two typos I
just missed and not an urge to run
some novel verbal marathon.' He might
reply, 'My long lines were a try
at showing poetry is still not prose, however
long the line and to avoid the slashes
which Olsen thought pauses for breath.'
I nod, 'I've used slashes, too, but not
for that, just to intensify
and quicken the pace.' We would
be getting on quite well by then. 'Someday,'
I'd say, 'I would like to read you, but
of course now there is my current worry
that influence might be retrospective,
and that I'll recognise your hand
in everything I've written, anyway.' He'd say,
'I don't think it's likely – aren't
you more into the lyrical? You look
sort of more lyrical but that
might be the light.' I would wonder: have I
aged back to O'Hara's age? He died
before he turned forty and maybe
one ages to the time and company.
Or maybe there are such lost creatures
as poets and each meeting each at first
in any place is nervous and newborn,
under erudite, angry cover. My daughter
thought the critic was doing the haka. I
might have done the haka with O'Hara
had I read him, but in the ever
new American night I would rather we
still sat there still, regaining self-
sense outside the great archives of torture.

Jennifer Maiden

Did you mean *iteration*?

The gmail interpolators algorithm my message to be about love
    poetry
They are wrong, all it is is
That I sent you a poem and said
love in my signoff.
To put the two together, presumptuous much, huh!
Machines – like data amoeba – sit back on their clever heels
    and think they are all smugly knowing about love.
They are not.
Even HAL, you do not get this even though you hung out with
    those guys for ages.
In Japan they labour yet to create these feeling machines
Always careful of the uncanny valley
And it wasn't until I was ensconced in your circular screen that
    I realised
When the trance soundtrack kicked in and the small images
    spun like the
Talking rings
That I realised this was the technology you had developed
This was the sphere you had written
The code for, in the all-encompassing round
My mind took off in some various syntheses as I realised how
    conversant we are.
I could recognise you,
by the concept.

Melinda Bufton

Disappearing Act

for Bas Jan Ader (1942–1975)
'because gravity overpowers me'

Things tilt,
                    fall
over and we
do: stasis a moment
before the forwards-

          jolt.
          In a slippery-shingled world
gravity became your ludic conspirator:
your *avant* heavy with visions
of afterwards.

Your early work
charts falls: 'Broken Fall (organic)' from a bike
into an Amsterdam canal;
'Broken Fall' into a trestle;
from a chair perched
on the roof, becoming
again the bundle your mother
threw to make
an impossible escape. 'Fall I'
Los Angeles 1970
can neither forget nor recall
Winschoten 1944.

For you at two
your father's execution
meant only abandonment.
Resistance, courage, harbouring

the persecuted: ideas beyond
the world of your days.
The words of your work collect
a toddler's small syllables:
PLEASE DON'T LEAVE ME

Later, a film so stark
(then a postcard, another
film, a photo)
that unstopped tears
collect all tears:
I'm too sad to tell you:
testimony of one who saw
but could not phrase:
particles of innocent witness.

And learning through this
grief's isolation
and the falling of all art:
thoughts unsaid
then forgotten

At the end
in Search of the Miraculaous:
a lonely voyage to
         break a-
cross
      the Atlantic
          fall into the vanishing point
no roof, windows
tilt, no earth

      all
        tilt: the sea's windows
opening to the miraculous.

(Note: Dutch-born conceptual artist Bas Jan Ader disappeared at sea during a solo voyage and artwork called 'In Search for the Miraculous'.)

Felicity Plunkett

Drowning dream

That August I began to dream of drowning. It was the season of water – strange storms troubled the air. All day I crept along the edges of rooms, avoiding the precious windows – half ajar, propped open with old newspapers – where the green sky pooled. Outside, whole oceans flooded the garden, encroaching on the house and its sagging porch. On the first floor the eaves – swollen, bloated with salt. On the second the mirrors, weeping sodden light; the carpets stained with moisture. On the third I studied the ceiling for cracks through which the rain might bloom. The attic and the landing damp. The skirting and the sideboards. The clocks. Only once (in the afternoon) I moved down to the basement, where a man – quiet and still as a mouse – floated face-down in the dark. Above us, the house hummed like a machine.

Bella Li

Dual Citizen

1 Pass

Jus sanguinis, law of blood
              as if by transfusion
you lived on, involuntary vampire,
                    I carry
by former marriage a mantle
you never wanted –
              Swiss Australian –
wherever you lived,
              you did not belong,
                    were the black sheep,
                    scapegoat.
Is this what you
                    impart, what I
              inherit?

2 Assisted Passage

Lobbed across continents
with a sweetheart on the SS *Sydney*

COME TO SUNNY AUSTRALIA!

                    no word of English but
this is the house that Jack built

lodged in a Nissen hut,
                    set to cut
lengths of metal
              for a suitcase company
in a country that didn't rate

immigrant degrees,
         making a new start.

3. Homeless

Later, when all fell apart:
                              off out of the
Marital Home and all alone,
                         cramming
into your Charger,
           lairy car she called the *death trap*, dossing
on back seat, teacher now—my teacher
                                for a while there
though I didn't know where
                    you were living
              planning your classes and marking
on front seat,
            washing in beachside blocks, moving on,
til when we met again
            in my twenties
                       you'd holed up
in a caravan with just room enough to stretch out –
                   how could I not let you in?

4 Expired

Red compacts, marked
with a little white cross,
           discarded,
                     old entities
in the bedside drawer:
                   am I still the bearer?
I own each particular.
Each unused LEAVE TO ENTER.

Acknowledge derivative status,
canton
        where I was never born
            and had never been,
cold northern town
of your first known ancestor
                mine
by assertion –
        a woman takes her husband's
Place of Origin, in the Swiss system –

handed on, in this wise
to my children's children,
        with no Swiss 'in' them,
IDs accreting,
        cancelling and slashed,
buried now among piles
           of underwear,

sketches for a portrait, Wildean,
that cannot flatter;
        the stages of breakdown.

How lightly I thought to cast it all off!
There's this whole other apparatus
           that wants to track me,
my *representation*,
that notes all my sins in the context
        of civil status
           and translates them.

5 Origins

Bülach, Bürgerort, is up near the border
almost off the map.

I've no real business here, revisiting,
kicking down streets I barely remember
              and that never knew me.

You hadn't been there either,
just learnt by rote the family lore:
Place of Origin means
              if we are ever destitute, we claim
              this right: they have to take us in.

You were always losing your foothold,
the very roof over your head,
                            your good
schoolmaster-father
              Swiss-village pillar
somehow ruined,
                      so that when we toured
so many years later, you showed me
two childhood homes: Before and After.

Then on to the school for boys
who 'sensed a vocation', under the chill
watch of that Black Madonna,
                            her foot
kissed so often it had worn down
like a patient child,
                      bearing Einsiedeln,
place of the hermit,
                      alone in a crowd.

6 Absolved

You were vowed to the Lord
                            and enrolled
to spread his Word:

Missionshaus,
Maria-Enzersdorf, in Vienna.

Always Maria,
substitute mother.

When they expelled you
after many years
(you who'd been telling,
townsfolk *Priests can't really forgive your sins*)

you went back to find your cell stripped
and reassigned.

For months you slept
in an attic, fed by a soft-hearted nun
who brought secret plates from the kitchen
that was trying to starve you out.

Did you think of Bülach then,
with nowhere to turn,
knowing that shame meant your parents' door
was closed forever?

7 Outsider

The real Bülach is starkly quiet as
I scout around it,
looking for
nothing. I head across town
and a young man,
thinking me English, warns,
'But Fraülein,
that is the *Catholic* church!'

Tracy Ryan

Dust

When I came back
after almost a month away
a wild wind had damaged the roofs of the neighbours' houses
and brought down the cherry laurel in our yard
and there was a fine layer of dust over everything: dust
in the cupboards, dust in the drawers, dust beneath the dried,
    cut roses,
the dust of our neighbours, the dust of the city, the dust
of the Simpson Desert
two thousand kilometres west.

What's there to say?

Sometimes, as I talk, I feel the dust
creeping through my sentences, thoughts
turning to fine powder
as they wend through the motes of it:
theories, philosophies, histories. Our dreams
are dust, our loves
are dust, the things
we fight for are dust.

In the Taj Mahal
they are sweeping the dust; in the Pentagon,
the Vatican. In the Louvre
they are brushing it
from the face of *La Gioconda*. In Padna
Emeliano is ploughing the dust; on the Hay Plain the sheep
are straggling through dust; in Canberra
the Prime Minister is coughing
because of the dust.

In the evening the dust
turns red in the sunset: there are
worlds up there,
and centuries, huge
cathedrals, great
archives of dust.

Sometimes,
when the wind dies,
you can hear the birds
crying
because of their burden of dust: crying
or singing, I don't know (the world
flows
through the dust of us,
sometimes it sings).

David Brooks

Earth Hour

It is on our hands, it is in our mouths at every breath, how not
remember? Called back
to nights when we were wildlife, before kindling
or kine, we sit behind moonlit
glass in our McMansions, cool
millions at rehearsal
here for our rendezvous each with his own
earth hour.
       We are feral
at heart, unhoused creatures. Mind
is the maker, mad for light, for enlightenment, this late admission
of darkness the cost, and the silence
on our tongue as we count the hour down – the coin we bring,
long hoarded just for this – the extended cry of our first coming
to his ambulant, airy
Schatzkammer and midden, our green accommodating tomb.

David Malouf

Edith

1.

When I was between eleven and twelve, my thin body
stooped slightly. My family took the matter in hand.
An orthopaedic manufacturer, an immensely fat gentleman,

the colour of a November fog, constructed for me a
    prison of iron.
Under my arms were thick pads of leather, reminiscent of saddlery.
My arms were constantly numbed. When I went to bed, my legs

were immured in a contraption of steel. I could not move.
My feet were strapped down onto a kind of steel sandal
    with a most
complicated lock and key system, four inches deep under
    the soles.

Sometimes Miss H screwed them into a position pointing
    downwards
and the discomfort kept me awake all night. Sometimes they
    pointed
heavenward, and the same pain happened. Impossible

for me to have left my bed, even if the room was on fire.
My only happiness was that during the day I was able to secrete
a book of poems in the fastnesses of my bed. I learned Pope,

Shelley, Shakespeare in a profound secrecy, hurriedly and
    guiltily,
by the light of a single brightly-feathered candle, whilst outside,
the seas of beauty, the wildness of the spring, broke upon a
    magical shore.

2.

A long train journey back to a ravaged capital,
in a compartment with three badly burnt airmen.
The pointed smell of antiseptic cream.

Out the window, the manicured and scarred hills,
green hills of England. One soldier has lost
his nose and lips, his face a terrible blankness.

He is quiet the whole time, doffs his hat as you leave.
Later, in a journal, the words appear –
What woman could ever be worthy to love him?

3.

Until she has made a technique for herself (and one has to
      forge it
for oneself, there is no help to be got), any woman, if she is
      going
to be any good at all, must write in as hard and glittering a
      manner

as possible, with as strange images as possible (strange but
      believed in).
Anything to avoid that ghastly wallowing. Deformation or
distortion in art is a necessary quality. Not only is this not a
      defect,

it is one of the sources of pleasure and interest. I was not
      pretending
to put forward a new theory of the universe – I was just
doing technical feats of an extreme difficulty and having fun.

Oh, why won't people realise poetry is a specialist's job! Always
I have been a little outside life, like a ghost, a dead person.
When I was very small I began to see the patterns of the world,

the images of wonder and I asked myself why they should be
    repeated –
the feather and the fern and rose and acorn in frost on the
    window,
repeated again and again. Even then I knew this was telling us
    something.

    4.

The engine, steaming. In the headlights, someone
is finishing off the howling alsatian who leapt
inexplicably from the bushes into the path of the car.

A slight tremor, you slowly realise is your body.
The dreadful silence pressing in.
When the car gets underway again, you speak

loudly about poets and composers, as if
your heart was not left there beside that road,
black tree wishing birds to land in your branches.

Back at the house, a large owl has come
to live in a courtyard, and in the morning,
it is one huge graveyard of the bones of mice.

Andy Jackson

Ellipsis

Rain streaks the window. Somehow her hair
holds the smell of matches struck.

The wind is loose around walls outside, tying itself
up in trees (birch leaves soft as ash).

She watches: breath showing and fading on glass.
He said *if,* and she waits, not knowing his language,

all the things he might have meant.

Jo Langdon

from Ephemeral Waters

Rocky   She starts in a trickle
Mountains
National   a rill
Park

                    a thread of water
Colorado   you can easily straddle, if only
River   you walk so far—
Trail

           she starts miles out beyond road
upstream   far enough that only river lovers
                  river readers

           might follow the scent
         might find source

yet on the trail upriver I meet
      them all—

           Just yards along the path
young families

         toddlers helped uphill
           by sibling hands until
         they've seen the water and turn back

further along, small groups, all groups
         out for an afternoon stroll, ripples of trios
and couples   Alone I overhear

their small talk, return a nod of the head
         as I pass with a faster gait until, miles further
toward the source day-hikers break

for lunch at missing Lulu City
　　　—while the city is gone
the vista remains

Water just covers my feet
　　　　the rocks of the streambed bloom
in orange and lilac

and I use the snow-melt flow to cool
　　　　my bottle　　　I watch
as every few yards

　　　　another
　　　　　　unmarked
　　　　unmapped runnel
　　　　　　choirs
　　　into
　　　　　　the gaining
　　　stream

　　　　　　　*

Soon *upriver* becomes
　　　　upstream
　　　　　　up
　　　　　　trickle

source　　　　When through rock I spy the seep

there's nothing to do but turn back
downstream　　　retrace the downward flow

A mile downstream again, water at ankle
　　　　She pools, climbs, carries
modest skirts onward

{64}

Another mile, water laps at my knee
　　　　again walkers spray
across the trail　　　Their clusters

ooh and *aah* at the pines
　　　　the mountain columbines
at each ascent
　　　　　　descent
　　　the rough trail makes

　　　Some hatless
in sandals and fluorescent shirts

others, grubby, well-kitted
　　　　　　　　each visible limb
brown enough to recede into tree

while along the streambed green
　　　　runs the gamut, olive- to bottle-
A modest start, gathering water

　　　—gathering, gathering—

sweeping along the banks of buried history
　　　　arriving again
Lulu　　　at the ghost of Lulu City
City

Kate Middleton

Five Abstractions of Blue

1. Prussian Blue

It is the dense compression of glaciers
that the artist has seized for his paint.
It lives as a flame's after-image
on a plain wall.
It is *The Great Wave off Kanagawa,*
der Werff's *Entombment of Christ*
and the colour of Mary's grief.

2. Refugee

Not night but the inside of a darkened cell
where every murmur of a life has been stilled,
minutes hanging on reinforced glass
like droplets smeared by a child—
or someone peering into a lake
at restless fronds of weed
standing in refracted haze—
an afternoon as blue
as a faded willow-pattern cup
on a rickety shelf;
as blue as dementia that has let go
of all detail except a child's slow climb
up the rungs inside a well—
the blue-white
of that waiting circle of light.

3. Plumber

Here is a bubbling drain
and a main adjoining pipe.

His eel wriggles towards
a cliff-face's stain of seepage
into an ocean basin.
He stands facing the horizon.
There is blue wherever he looks—
even the horizon
is crossing out of purple,
as if sunset is siphoning day
into an estuary
on the other side
of his blinking observation.
He thinks of the vast flow,
the possible backwash,
the way he stands now in the offing
of that ensconced and draining light;
of his embayment
in the reaching, shallow glow,
its impressionistic shoal.

4. Paragliding

Up here she is in free fall;
up here the wind catches her dropping spiral
and fills her parafoil; up here
she turns across
the shattered rectangles of ground—
all that fuss of traffic and laws
and her unsteady, deflating marriage
dissolved in gravity's tug
and the wind's upthrust. The sky
is thrall and abeyance
and a dense, yellowing blue
that absorbs her ascent;
her single, teardrop wing
stiffened against its harness.

5. Indigo

Soak the leaves
until they ferment, mix lye.
Follow the way of ancestors;
make cloth that has always been made.
Dress in blue. Don't stand
in the vat during pregnancy.
Look to alter your life.
Escape from the people who claim you
and the village and towns you know.
Set out in the colours you have.
Remove them. Stand in the rain.
Wash your hands in the sea.
Wear the dust of the ground,
the light of the indigo sky
in every elaborate weather.
Notice the blue of your veins.

Paul Hetherington

Five Deaths

Et ce monde rendait une étrange musique,
Comme l'eau courante et le vent.
                    —Baudelaire, 'Une Charogne'

"four out of five times
they sop Holidays
or piss forty years with
bright attention.

clots glide about
like snails: they'll see it
happen, left arm thrilling
before the samsung,

helpless with understanding.
i can't fathom the brain's
betrayal, how our coral or
polyp selves would watch,

abet. the body unseen before
us; one of Freud's nude dogs,
not pretty or alive, but definitely
stuff, dōgen wonders on mount hiei

why look? then, living, plunges
into the yellow springs! some
refuse food, its meaning
cleft, their thirties invisible

for the native arrangement.
naturally, not even their names
waiting behind like eggs, we all
worried the box precisely.

but once"

Tim Grey

Floored

after Henry Moore

Mother draws the clock down
with her eyes
asks me gently.

Knuckles blanching I work from her nape
to the ball inside her shoulder.

Lunch rings a little bell –
my fingers blink

across the plains her tread
like cloud shadow.

Dropping
her nightdress darkens;
she never drowns but makes another cliff.

Bonny Cassidy

Francis Webb at Ball's Head

Sandstone dust swirled into the westerly
and settled off Ball's Head; the shark
rose from its rock, then slid into Berrys Bay.

Gliding towards the deep water.
Francis watched the artist who carved it
'brush death from his wits' again.

The windy sky stretched before him
and his old interlocutor, the sun, flared
on the windscreens of cars cruising the road
near the council fence in need of paint.

Francis knew time as a whirlpool.
He sees the old baker's horse he loved, swishing
its tail, flies on its back, the oily harness.

The straightjacket and regimental clock
swing through the night of his dream
and a shark from this harbour-dreaming.

He watches the carcass of the old horse
as it is over-run by taunting boys
pulling a dead tail, the black mane.

In the landscape of his mind language gathers
in storm clouds, the lightening
carves grooves in sandstone; waves break
on the oily rocks, full of sparks.

The city surrounds the harbour, electric
with clarity, the tide's indigo mirror.

The leathery wings of flying-foxes
across centuries, out from the glow.

Seagull-shit streaks the coal wharf
white flakes on pylons reflect the tug-light.
Francis runs his fingers across the shark.

Night, hard night. Young homeless men
around a drumfire making pea and hambone soup
with their last few pence.

Light from Pinchgut, above a swimming convict,
catches batwings, a sea-mullet in mid leap,
the ghost of a grey-nurse in Grandfather's sails.

Channels, the lead-line, corks. Difference
with the dark of the moon and the hatched whitebait.
The Head is alive.

Robert Adamson

"Hindley Street"—How to be perfect there

Pete Bakowski's challenge: attempt Padgett's 'How To Be Perfect'.

"Hindley Street"—
I write those words, the
title of this poem,
on this pad,
to start a list—*of things I must
do.* Is this
going to be a poem?
Isn't it?
("Hindley Street"—
I know what it will mean.
I continue the list …
Names of people I should
email. Richard, in case
my silence is taken to mean something,
something dark, brooding—
Micky, to break *her* silence.)

Different from what I had been
going to write—fired up
by the fetishized nebulosity
of the Houynhhyms last night.

I get a haircut instead,
& the head massage that
goes with it
syphons off
all anxiety.
Philosophers,
rub your heads!

My hair short again—
my visage modern.

Now, to work—
to face down the future
as it comes on
like gangbusters,
minute by minute—
doing this & doing that—
philosophy, meanwhile, on the back-burner.
Simmering.
I add Simryn Gill
to the list. Hullo, Richard, Micky, Simryn!

Like a small-minded Frank O'Hara,
a sort of contradiction in terms—

small-minded then, not like Frank O'Hara,
but with my haircut, at least,
ashamed of a century that is
ashamed of me, if it thinks about it.
Me, & the century—at neither of which
I can smile. Time to get
my head rubbed? *No time for that*—
the future arriving incrementally,
minute by minute—
like pirates boarding a ship.
So it's Game On!

I rather like the look
of this loony tune
swinging in the rig, his earrings
& bandanas, cutlass
between his teeth.
Tho is it Peter Bakowski,

in disguise, this pirate
'of the future'—forget
I ever said that!
(The future
can look after itself.) ? —
is it Peter?
& the pirate hands me a
telegram from, let's see…
H.G. Wells? Herbert
'Vere' Evatt? Someone
futuristic—
Arnold Schwartzenegger!?—
no—Ron Padgett.
The pirate now looks like Ron,
I note,
as I read the letter, look up to his
face—which nods, lips parted,
still breathing heavily,
full of encouragement—
& read again.
It says, You've forgotten
to read the instructions—haven't you?
"What?" I say, I think.
Ron speaks:
"*How To Be Perfect*—
it was in my book of the same name.
I know you've read it—
and Kenneth Koch, his 'General Instructions', 'The
Art Of Love', and other poems-of-advice.
But you don't seem to have
taken it all in. Or you
bracket it off, as if it
weren't real life. We're
not fooling about, buddy.
Sure, make a list of things to do.

You've got that right.
But put the right things on the list!
'Get a haircut'? Why not?
But is that gonna solve anything?
And if you're gonna get a haircut
Get the Right Haircut—
you look like a disaster!
Sure, write to your friends,
that's a good idea.
And if you're dealing with Hounyhymms
Take some energy from the encounter—
You've got that right! But ...
must you deal with them at all?
Or are you not very discriminate
in your use of the term? Were they
that bad? Ask yourself this.
The future is neither
your friend nor your
enemy unless you set it up that way.
A few precautions, that's
my advice. Like
Peter Bakowski, he's got it right.
We're not a bunch of pirates—
(yes, I'm from the future—
your future, anyway—
it may not be so bleak)
I dress like this
to get your attention.
I'm normally a sneakers-&-jeans
kind of guy, I wear my cap
facing forwards,
over a closely cropped head,
with my signature round glasses.
Not this pirate crap. How they
ever got about, in all this gear,

is hard to figure. But the future
is not *waves of pirates*
boarding your ship. You're a
glass-half-empty kinda guy,
aren't you? You & Tony Towle
take it on the chin—*for*
preference, don't you? You
think that's 'Romantic Irony'?
You're an Australian—
what's romantic about that?
Have you written to Tony lately?
    You haven't written to me.
So, make a list!
I don't hold out much hope for you.
You should maybe
re-read my books.
That might help. And Peter Bakowski's,
he's the man.
And here our conversation broke off
near the knoll's island foam.

Ken Bolton

Hotel

In the swish hotel lobby

flight attendants do a kind of happy dance.

Freshly showered and shaved,

they are ready for the airport bus.

Then it's up, up and away:

Champagne, smoked salmon

and stroking for first class,

a smile and mixed nuts for economy.

Outside, life bats the double glazing

like a summer blowfly.

Near the gleaming brass revolving door

a man and his dog are camped.

There's water in a stainless steel bowl,

a corrugated placard describing hard luck,

and an upturned hat with a smattering of coins.

Next to him a cleaner polishes his pane.

Mark Mahemoff

Ich Möchte: A Monument to My One Date with J. Robert Oppenheimer's Granddaughter in Santa Fe, New Mexico, 1987

Infinitesimally by zit
nucleic chitchat
got spoke in our Trinity
of larges:

cherry-lime sodas, chilli
cheese fries
we ordered to split
in the huge

teenage Friday jalopy –
engineering
we couldn't un-chain, reverse
out of, undo

that night, *Desperately Seeking
Susan*'s innuendo
me, she formed invisible umlaut
dropped on

her Grandfather's verbs
to die, to want
conjugation I'd later
fail
to pronounce

plans for a sequel

Kent MacCarter

In the Desert

)))
)))
)))
)))
)))
)))
)))
)))
)))
)))
)))
)))
)))
)))
)))
)))
)))
)))
)))
)))
)))
)))
)))
)))
)))
)))
)))
)))
)))
)))

R. D. Wood

Induct True Legendary Thrills Bravery

Bravery captors medal heroism circulate mission leftovers
Bravery tracks the saddle that throws sad off backs as
Honour full bloods across country's rescues
Replica escorted stream afield sees gallantry
Dark men more inspectors arrested in love
Cross Excellency gives the saving life's points.
Convey roads typical ways, neighbour often
Parcel swam opposite devotion
Dragging semi-mounted charges, we miles
Loud conscious after the midstream sank hesitate
Brow broad uniform bronze inch by heights
The trunk inscription assembled appears
The oval mouth publicly saved clan Khaki piece strays apart of
    inaugurate
Stage by age the presentive speaker a trust defined name so nameless
Grand assault step no corner mental façade private.
Bravery nutritional fluffy batter artificial voice
Sang cholesterol delicious as beer wept we to we lightly to ingredients
The coward added.
Fairytale mind games got, titanium webbed revenge
So frocked that an angelic to fabulous secret shock catchy tunes.
Maids melodramatic men's nuptials a series nighttimes soapie.
Perfect bravery became pictures vows room Chantilly bridal votive
    smiles.
Idol dolls Idol dollars slip trimester
Captor audition gentle massaged newly wedded
Track smooches arrival ivory hype emotional
Attention bar tab bravery
Replica escort love's blood laws lawless
Stream afield flirt stay flirt goes.
Rebel the bells licence amorously bravery.

Lionel G. Fogarty

Inside Edward Hopper

Room in New York, 1932
We are in the front room upstairs. Just your usual rented brownstone.
Apart from the piano. We only came to look at art and now we're
inside a painting, held by the dark frame of the window at night.
He's not talking to me. He's posing, pretending to read, stretching
the paper into black and white shapes. I tinkle a few notes. Waiting.
Electric light can be so brittle. It sharpens the space between us. My
red dress has become the focal point in the picture, flesh tones soft
against mahogany. Some guy is watching from the apartment across
the street. He thinks I haven't noticed. I should pull the drapes,
block out his angle of vision. But then we'd never get out.

Nighthawks, 1942
There's no stopping him: he went off in the middle of the night.
Said he was going out for cigarettes. I'm not in this picture. There's
no door, so I don't know if I could get in. Or how he will get out!
He's sitting in there smoking, watching the couple at the counter,
well the redhead anyway. The waiter is making small talk. Passing
time. They are all shaped in a diner window. Separate, like extras
in a movie. Artificial light freezes the frame, draining the colour.
He's always looking for the story beyond the painted surface. But
this time he's gone too far.

Brenda Saunders

Jivin' With Bonny Cassidy etc.

never the same
        night—never the same
            light in the feet
dark devil in the heel

the dress got wet—
        i cut it off—i lost
            control—rolled off the bed
                //

the fault was all stylus—
        how it beat the rhythm out
           the groove—flicked
        the heel
           'cross the boards of the J.C. Hotel—
        shaking, grinding
           skip, kick & flack
                tr

specifics track the mental map
        of a night well spent—
           … dot is the line that solves two points
           heel to   heel

      play it loud,   *louder again*

the dress got wet—
        i cut it off
        i lost
           control—
            //

the drink sunk in—

             i swigged the heat
drew out   the sweat
          slips down the arcing spine—
               shredded moments in a salt-licked
                         time—

viscous liquids all shook up
          in the dense light of a dusky pub—
the buddy system—lava lamp
that won't dissolve

          louder,   *louder still*

the dress got wet—
          i cut it off
          i los   t control—
                    //

mischief can't control her hands—
          i stole the gin—
               four fingers
               down their throats—
               and one was mine
               and it was cut

                         (signals to the floor—
                                   a point
                                        two
          bodies in a field—free-spinning dandelion drift
                    matching feet
bonny lass,
               bonny class
                              bonny stylus groove
|| :
the dress got wet— ·

```
        i cut it o  ff
        i lo  st  cont
                    rol
                            : ||
                    fell off the bed

and bonny laughing out the window
        says "come on let's go—
```

Jessica L. Wilkinson

Last Goodbyes in Havana

After Carver

Midday cracks like a cool blue cup.
We drink a last rum among the tanned couples
and kiss pre-revolutionary glass to our lips,
smooth and honest and scratchless.
Beneath us, waves smash the Malecon
with a force that could break our lives.
Your eyes are hidden behind your sunglasses.
Your hand shakes. Now and then you turn a page
of *The Dangerous Summer* and sigh
accusingly. We have cheated, certainly. Lied.
Days we have fought float over us effortless
as grease. Soon I will take a night flight to the Pacific
and in Manhattan a woman is waiting
who you have taught more than enough
about patience and her possible life.
You tap your knife against your plate
and turn a page. Down the cliff, Cuban boys
are diving off the stonewall into distance.
Their young bodies gleam with promise.
They kick down, then rise from the water like seals.

Sarah Holland-Batt

Le Cimetière du Montparnasse

I was almost drifting up the avenue
leading to the tomb of Baudelaire.
Names were flowing back into my mind –
my year in Paris 1959 –
Sartre, Ionesco, Jouve and Ponge –
when suddenly I saw a quiet group
looking for some place they could not find.
It proved to be the grave of Vallejo.

Who were they, self-contained and whispering,
students, fellow poets, refugees?
I'm sure they must have been Peruvians,
they knew his work, his worth, his world.
They crossed themselves, and stood there, full of care.

Vivian Smith

Leçons de Ténèbres

But are they lessons, all these things I learn
Through being so far gone in my decline?
The wages of experience I earn
Would service well a younger life than mine.
I should have been more kind. It is my fate
To find this out, but find it out too late.

The mirror holds the ruins of my face
Roughly together, thus reminding me
I should have played it straight in every case,
Not just when forced to. Far too casually
I broke faith when it suited me, and here
I am alone, and now the end is near.

All of my life I put my labour first,
I made my mark, but left no time between
The things achieved, so, at my heedless worst,
With no life, there was nothing I could mean.
But now I have slowed down. I breathe the air
As if there were not much more of it there

And write these poems, which are funeral songs
That have been taught to me by vanished time:
Not only to enumerate my wrongs
But to pay homage to the late sublime
That comes with seeing how the years have brought
A fitting end, if not the one I sought.

Clive James

Little Book of Mourning

i.m.JHH

Winter

Dark freeze in Charlottesville;
The drinking water's grown small teeth.

Bare room: I write till dusk
In dusty radiator heat.

Clocks graze on me all day;
I hear the silence of two crows

Then look down at my arm:
Not even your shadow's there to touch.

Inside

I only speak old words:
They keep in with the dead,
They leave their doors ajar.

Some words are corridors
That lead us to the dead
And we can trust their dark;

We pass a hammer, sure,
We pass an anvil too
We pass a stirrup last;

And then we find the dead
Curled up, inside, asleep,
With our names on their tongues.

On the Mantelpiece

My father doesn't know
That he died years ago:
He looks out for a while

From 1965 or so
And I look back, although
It chills away my smile

To see him with a glow
At dinner, in the snow,
In full-on sixties style

Not knowing then the blow
That was to knock him low,
And scrapes me like a file.

Parachuting

They dropped you into France when young
A town up north (I went there once);

Your squad was braced behind a wall
And you could see the man up front

Go left and his big head go right
And you threw up, you said, and ran

Across the street when shouted there
And fell down too, no time at all.

You showed me medals only once
And a weird wound just once as well,

A mucky hole that sucked in flesh
On each side of an upper thigh.

Now you've gone down again at night:
No river and no fields beneath.

Downstairs

I walk down there
Because I must
And feel each step
Is less than just

And blank a thought
But can't ignore
A shadow's sigh
The furnace roar

This is the place
Where darkness grows
This is the place
My father goes

Kevin Hart

Loans slip

Perfect phrases for the sales call :
50 things you want to know about world issues and
How to survive without a job : practical
Working overseas : a working holiday guide /
Why men earn more : the startling truth behind
Leadership for dummies /
What's eating your child? : the hidden connections between food and
Money and soul : the pyschology of money and the transformation of
House rules /
The alchemy of finance : reading the mind of
Consulting for dummies /

Jane Gibian

Lumière train

I'm sitting by the silvery train tracks, under the moon, in a
    leafy auditorium.
Tons of steel and light approach from the wings of the stage
and thunder through with warm flashes of amber luminescence:
the train windows, shaped like animatic frames of old film-reel
    negative,
flicker by at 18 frames a second.
Just enough to bring the commuters back to life

Darby Hudson

Marrickville

Later that night, I cut
the plastic boning from the bodice of my dress:
no need for structure, over summer.
There were bruises
on my knees I didn't recognise.

I saw us all that day, all day
projected on a big screen:
        the bathtub underneath the orange tree,
crushed grass imprinted on my shins,
your cat-like eyeliner, the warm
sangria out of mugs. My feet grew numb
beneath my hips. Saturation.
                I still felt overseen

when I walked home, alone and shouldered.

A black light flicked behind a balcony,
a woman, neon-lit,
        crushed out a cigarette
and turned to kiss, to give
a kiss. It takes

three keys to open my front door.

Fiona Wright

Mateship

Was it eupepsia? I wasn't thinking:
Why does everything have to be such a rush.
Or the mottled weather? I wasn't even
wondering how indignant to be about what
when the media and self-interest provide
reasons to keep me indignant all the time.
Walking to the station, I had a vague sense
of what it might mean to feel real affection
for the things — the patterns of energy-stuff —
in the world, and, being one such or many
myself, to adjust them here and there in right
but unnecessary ways. The shadow-pools
in the street seemed continuous with a night

like a party spilling from a mansion split
into flats along a canal, an open-
ended night full of divergent adventures,
novelty lamps, doors ajar, strange languages
and splashes. Then a vaguely familiar guy
with his elbows out came up to me and said
"Usually I think, Life will sort you out, mate,
but this time it looks like life has to be me."

Chris Andrews

Mediterranean Time

The swarthy plumber who sets a time
to fix the taps never comes. Water
drips in nearby limestone caves
with less regularity from stalactites.
Church bells clang, now in a frenzy,
then once only and, much later, once again –
shuttered solitude now in silent streets
during the heat of the afternoon. In the shade,
on dusty ground, thin cats yawn.
Hibiscuses expose their sexy throats.
Should the plumber come, after
a siesta's done, he'll likely find
no-one home. He may later phone.
The sun shines hard on a limestone landscape
from which, block by sawn block,
the villages have risen as did – but how? –
megaliths during the Neolithic.
There's no division of colour, honeyed,
between what's man-made and the land –
the villages often atop the coralline-
capped mesa-like formations.
They look down on tiers of ancient cultivation.
Olive lizards spurt in and out
of the drystone walls – a species
endemic to the island after the sea
gushed into the Mediterranean basin
with cataclysmic swiftness.
The Romans called the landfall Gaulus.
Its stratified cliffs are the Miocene
made scenic. Marine fossils
in a fanned museum line up
under glass, put a contemporary shine

on geologic time; another case displays ancient bones.
Perhaps of a distant, distant forebear
of the plumber who, in this farrago,
shrugs off haste, short north of the cliffs.

Andrew Sant

Meeting the Relatives

They're on you before you know it,
careering around the corner in that
flashy ball of light – curious, energetic
and eager to share the fun. You're it.
Is that really you lying by the television or
slumped in the front seat, still alive?
You reach for a phone to call your mother
but she's saying don't worry darling,
I'm here, peeling away from your astonished
face another translucent mica flake.
There are layers of faces within you now,
each one vibrant with self-determined life,
fascinated by your stories, waiting their
turn to speak. You settle back painlessly
knowing the news can't be all bad, it's past!
These people you're descended from, who seem to
know you, are saying that they own you
as you float on your back in champagne,
their faces are thought bubbles, popping
your elevated, delighting brain.
A voice deep inside you, which could
be your own, is saying *Let's Go* ...

Richard Kelly Tipping

Meeting with the Same River

In the spring I met with the afternoon of the same river

When I found that the sorrow inside its body

And the hidden language of its gestures

Were surprisingly similar to someone else's tragedy

Once I went so far as to open my mouth and speak the dead's
   secrets

In summer or even when it was colder

I kept silent or when I walked alone on the bank

The person who liked swimming at night

Acted the way a bird did in the water

On many occasions I go upstream along the river in search of
   a shoe

Because no one understands how to talk with the river

A lone snow crane on the water does not know whether to step
   forward or backwards

Bai Helin (translated by Ouyang Yu)

Melbourne ode

Melbourne, still home
to men with Spam-coloured
faces and no-coloured hair
who stand around on Fitzroy corners
waiting for the saloon-bar doors to swing
and hack away at winter mornings
with lungfulls of Holiday and Horizon
until the first cold Draught
hits the bottom of the glass
and who have never yet called home
on a smartphone.

Matt Holden

My Husband's Grave

I ripped a cotton thistle from the grass beside your grave.
No doubt you stepped on them on your last march,
pulled the spines from your trousers, admired the lovely
purple flowers. How far you walked, past burning haystacks
and deserted houses, past women who looked at you
and looked away. I'm sure you dreamt of the shady verandah
at home, bees flitting about the garden, my plum jam cooling
in the kitchen, a long letter safe in your overcoat pocket, a poem
written on the back of a handbill advertising cod-liver oil.
Your dear friend, Miklós Lorsi, was shot beside you,
the bullet slicing into his chin where he once rested his violin.
If you'd marched with the second unit you would have lived,
Miklós Radnóti, like your poems—poems the earthworms
did not eat; love as tough as a thistle and as hard to eradicate.

Andy Kissane

my singing empty hands

i hold the boat steady and my sister
climbs in   the boat smells of lavender
as only the image of a boat
can smell of lavender in a dream

        water purling at the lip   my sister
        has not grown any older
        my sister says
        i smell like garlic

my sister takes the oars
you sit she says *i row   don't you know*
anything?   my sister's words
smell strongly of washing powder

        she flinches when i touch her
        shut up she says *just let me row*
        my sister's hands on the oars
        smell of soap and some sinister

cheap perfume my daughter sometimes
wears when she is angry   my sister
closes her hands on the oars
my sister does not see me at all

        there's the smell of kelp in the water
        some rival in her head *do you remember*
        nothing she says *you say is true*
        i taste the snow in the air between us

my sister rows
precisely and with determination
the book grows soggy in her hand
ink   grass clippings   blood

        why aren't you helping she cries at last
        thrusting the oars at me as she sheds
        her crocodile tears *you never do anything*
        the book with which she has been rowing

from under her lashes my sister
watches me   my sister's tears
taste like lamingtons   my sister's voice
shines with the cut of scales

        my sister does not see through her crying
        the flash of real fish in the flashing water
        my sister sits in our small boat
        in the middle of that wide little water

with rounded shoulders
the smell of iron filings
something burning
she wears our mother's hair

Shari Kocher

Nostalghia

after Tarkovsky's Nostalghia

In sleep he is sent
to a memory that nears
its incarnation.
He can see his silhouette
in the distance,
it walks a dusk horizon
that curves like the top
of a molecule.

His real life earns
a passing mention
in a lengthy deposition
under hypnosis.

*

In the caverns of the baths,
in his clothes and shoes
Gorchakov walks through water;
there is all the difference in the world
between here and home
and as he wades
he smokes a cigarette.

Gorchakov is in danger.
He can be both
inhaled and blown away.
Rather than a reflection,
on a mirror he is condensation.

Sometimes he is just
the breath of a dog.

This poet is a photograph.
When the emulsion
of his thin silver present
is exposed to light, it channels
an old instinct's pictures.
His country has formed crystals.

*

At nineteen I was a receptionist
at a photographic college.
One of the students
was a man from the mines. He said
Where do accents come from?
      And I said something about
kinds of English sounds breeding along a line
– an auditory line of whomever ended
up in Australia, for instance.
In-bred voice noise.
And he said, *But at first?*
What is an accent in its own place?
It must be something in the rocks.

*

All the water in this film
is actually voice
that has decomposed.

In Gorchakov's head,
in moving countries he

has started a precipitation.
Think how Domenico's house leaks
even when it is not raining –
somehow, sonar has bled.

Gorchakov's old memory is animated
and it transitions through states.
A liquid distilled from his country
is in his blood.

                    *

At the moment of heart attack,
it is the gas of this country
that drifts from his mouth.

As the poet becomes unconscious
a stratum is formed
and in this layer
memory is a demon that walks
like a soldier from a tunnel.

Carmen Leigh Keates

Not in vain

You think of gracious ladies, I of gents: not so
young, dressed in rain. We are quiet, mad, like drummers looking
    for a band. We turn over the soil, marvel at
our tranquillity. All's well in Paris, according to
    the TV. Magic roofs of thatch have descended
creating brown shadows. A rustle and bark, but no
    dog in the yard. We've seen the international
children crying at the graves of Tutenkhamen. They're
    on tour like us. Cairo's Proust iguanas his gay
eyes, his gay neck. The sacred lawns are being mown. Mainland
    ways. Five minutes sunshine, then Fleur-de-Lys Island.
The attitude of the pottery up there's chilly. We
    throw rocks at its crimson calm. I'd come to imprint
the sky on my green-gold mind. At first I felt flush, vain
    boggled. Cooing images of the lotused ground.
Sunny creature, resting through spring ... grace to be visible.

Michael Farrell

Nyirbator

on top of the bridge
the danube's bullpit the mosquitoes
the brown stones the currency
accumulating everything as it should be and

hair emptying into a plastic bag
outside the synagogue my arm
itchy I pray for the return of
a name this is all so super it is
also regular and I see it as a bright
pink boarder or empty glasses frames
or a nut shell this is you watching me
behave like a nut shell entirely tied up
to some familiar name stoned marble
this is you petrified stoned palpable
the nut is no longer moved by stimuli
not even purple grapes or purple light
on barmitzvahed hands the most
precise siren is silence and if you
wander through the mass names and
rub your eyes is it because you are
expressing sadness or is it because
I happen to be playing with a name
as it used to be I do feel like I'm watching
you yes I am from a bridge do me a favour
visit my family tell me their names

Oscar Schwartz

Ochre

green and bright blue flits of colour
swirl in a mallee-grey underground
amid constant bird song harmony

along the riverbank bee eaters
dart rainbows around her head
as she paints her body with yellow ochre

splash crimson on bleeding eyes
through the tunnel of darkness
honour the dead

Ali Cobby Eckermann

Ode on Love

What he has taken of me
I don't even want back,
I don't want to want back.
This new happiness holds up
a novel mischief that waits in the near.
Why so indispensible?
Before I knew him I did not need him:
if he goes I must replace him,
as if I could. And that circling body-mashing doubt.
How he throws me
into dark and retrieves me!
And with gazes like little riffing flames inhabits me.

What does the bottom-most soul know of this –
that basin of us
concerned only with survival,
collecting residual passion
and washing clean,
shining up that bit of us
that cares nothing?

That idea that every lover is the same,
that there's a template, a type,
that what I call all-but-worship's not this man but an all-man man
likely to be just like my father:
being one man he is all,
many desires folded into one bright
bouquet of obsession that springs from the heart like Spring.

He is coasting along his own midnight.
The trapping of his breath, the only outward sign,
I devour it like meat,

as if it was him,
tenderly and watchfully in all love's creepiness.
Love is a thing, the self's
undoing that it begs for.
He twitches out hot shivers of love he shifts away from,
exalts and voids me
with the economy of a waiter emptying a whole table with one hand.

Power to love draws the long breath from me.
Petrarch made this a joy, an Other queening distance,
love never shaken by reality, never
whittled by exchange.
I fear whatever we have will puff like a daisy.
And if not?
Mutuality, mutability, love nuanced and grappled, hard.
This seam of encounters can't peg itself down,
it is or isn't, it is high or low, a scythe swinging in, or out.

The self tries to locate him, and itself
in all the moving signifiers of love,
lover and love, meaning and feeling,
things that says, love this one, not another.
I lie in bed scratching at the night.
Absent, his beauty
evaporates. He flickers before me,
knowable-unknowable, central lover, man-figure
skating so sweetly at the edge of a beauty.
How I hope against. How I want to know if he.
And love dares the self.
To risk what there is in hope of havocking more to risk.

Trying not to try to purloin him whole
but keep him near – to tell my heart so stupid!
The drawbridge clatters up.

Petra White

Old Europe (2)

You don't need to queue at the entrance
but then so dark your captions now unreadable
since the children left.
Come dine with me in a dead café.
Let's dance in my old Turkish residence
lined with uncut books
where a cigar accords with taste
and the chocolatier snores.
You may need to sidestep the urine.
Rémy flew home in a djellaba
the armless no glory veteran
the pigeons don't bother with the bread
the accordion's sellotaped to wheeze a tune.
The Romanies sell puppies to lovesick tourists
but the light is what we dream,
Saron's scything searchlight,
the Eiffel Tower a blingy earring
on the ear of Europa.
In the courtyard of a hôtel particulier
she showed me the seventeenth century
rainwashed and dishabille
with a horse in harness
and a Russian lover who won't spy for money or love.
A warning: the shih tzu twins are locked in
patrolling my millionaire terrace,
the road a crime scene below, a day-for-night
with Citroen and café shoot-out.
You might have to step over the body.
I only come here for summer,
for language, macaroons,
delicious cod. Good thing Cheryl

got the handbag she wanted she's
so persistent we filmed it.

Adam Aitken

On Dreams

It needs a strong will, and patience
to hold the dream inside the body
while the mind imprints itself with icons
of bright smoke, and an arm reaches for pen, paper.
Timed out, the dream's beyond reclaim:
a shoreline's wash of moon eclipsed by cloud.

A dream saved is this glass of water
which lights a piecemeal, bizarre version of a room,
encrypts and reverses a text in progress,
swells, presses flat, these fingertips.
As the day warms, the glass collects dust,
fresh shadows, kaleidoscopes gold air.
You sip from it, drinking the room, the dream:
here and now and then; nowhere, never.

Diane Fahey

On Not Getting my Spray Can Signed by Mr Brainwash

after Elvis *(2009), by Thierry Guetta*

It's not that I'd prefer
     another portrait of St. Michael
to Elvis wielding an M16
     designed by Fisher & Paykel.

Wait, I mean by Fisher Price –
     point being I appreciate
a top shelf Invader piece
     as much as any Eurydice,

and I'm pretty sure I get
     the way our fetishisation
of the toy assault rifle
     inflects his canonisation

as The King. It's just that capital
     encourages this: the endless
permutations of its effects
     are hardly less mindless.

The hubris is in thinking
     of each meme-savvy mashup
as a protest, allied to a flash
     mob trashing Topshop.

It's not. This canvas is passive
     as TV. No caulking with irony

can prevent its shtick's hull
       ripping on the reef of cliché.

I pray to Duchamp not to be
       the guy who cries *Scheissers!*
unfazed that he's conscripted
       by the thing he criticises.

Jaya Savige

Outstretched Arms

for Noel Rowe

maybe I'm getting used to it   the drive down the M5
black bitumen as smooth   as any beach
the search for parking   in Randwick   heels clicking
in hospital corridors   and my brother's
measured breath   intensive care is
quiet like a library   where machines and nurses
speak in lowered tones   as if death was sleeping nearby
not to be awakened   we're trying to talk to him
but it's hard to speak to stillness
the doctors keep saying   you must remember
his coma score   was very low
though young people often surprise us

my youngest brother   should be studying for the hsc
        according to my parents
instead he carts   his dreadlocks and skateboard
past hospital security   and tries to chat up
the pretty british nurses
I don't know how to comfort him when he starts crying
so we don't talk much   about the accident
or the operations   that aren't succeeding
instead we argue about the radio station   in the car
or we tell stupid stories   trying to capture moments
in nets of cynicism   and hard-eyed laughter

sometimes we offer   each other alternatives
I'd rather fail the hsc   I'd rather fail uni
than have a body   prised from a snarl of metal
lying silently beside me   perhaps we're each remembering
backyard games of cricket   in fading suburban light

or the three of us on bikes   weaving through
south coast scrub   on our way back to campfire & breakfast
     after one operation   the shunts probe
my brother's brain   to measure the pressure
the doctors tell us   that we each have an ICP of three
or six when we have a headache   now visiting time
is consumed by shifting numbers   that seem to be
always rising   like sydney real estate   or a bad economy
one day it goes up   to forty six
and I can hardly stand

when my mother was a child   all she wanted was a doll
instead of a school uniform   from a culture
that understood mixed business   more than Christmas
now she explores the hospital   to pass the time
finding all the cafeterias
the Eastern Suburbs views   that gaze out over her childhood
and the distant blue of Coogee   one day she walks
into a glass wall   thinking it's a door
that should automatically part   she isn't hurt
just dazed   and crying for hours   in the afternoon
a man sits   outside the hospital doors
sucking in smoke and weak sunshine   a day later his brother
stops breathing   he can't cope   when they turn
the machine off   so they have to call security
to pull him from the nurses   sometimes I think
     I'm not coping well either
giving shopkeepers the wrong money and showing up for
     classes
an hour early   a lady on the bus stares
out into Centennial park   what are we doing?
she asks of no-one   or everyone
I want to reply   but instead look down at my hands
rolling my bus ticket   and unrolling it again

as days click past   we're finding tragedy
in each waiting room   face   sharing stories
and cups of tea   over month-old wedding photos
where my brother grins   in forty degree heat
gripped by a suit & tie   and the speech he had to give
after the accident   they had to cut   his shirt off
my cousin returned it   along with his watch
she hadn't looked at   because someone said
if his watch is okay   then he'll be okay   every few days
another family leaves   after someone else drifts
out of the habit of living   they each wish us luck
as though death   were some blackjack game
and you have to know   when to quit the table

my father's got a bad habit   of leaving felt-tip pens
in his top pocket   so that they burst in the wash
most of his old shirts look like   he's been shot
in the breast   he writes down   the doctors' daily reports
in the same   steady hand he uses   to work through
maths problems   & calculations   for fluid mechanics
I don't read any of them though   afraid of seeing
an equation   that won't fall out   in a QED or answer
to be honest   I can't bring myself to read anything
at all at the moment   without feeling the weight
of a more urgent story   instead I try to line
my mind with   half finished crosswords
& whispered prayers   thrown skywards
longing for outstretched arms   and words
that european theory   declares meaningless

someone suggests we see a movie   to pass the time
        and to miss the easter traffic
in it   drew barrymore has lost her memory
and repeats one day   endlessly
it could be   the model for the way

adam sandler makes films
but my mother sobs   during all the jokes
imagining a different son   waking up
eyes glazed like hospital windows   I wonder if my brother
will remember Jesus   and that to die is gain

at the moment though   I'd rather the fruitful labour part
back on the dairy where farmhands sweat and swear
when cows won't shift   remember the suburban baptism
in front of smiling school friends?   cool water lapping
before plunging & rising   in a backyard pool
(salt water not chlorine)   under a grey sky at dusk
but now he's just floating   on his back
on a hospital mattress   sustained by breath
not his own   a family friend is
the chaplain at the hospital   one day he asks if he can
pray with us   over my brother
and anoint him with oil   it runs down my brother's
forehead like tears that stiches can't cover
someone at uni says   easter's the season for miracles
but more than three days have passed   and we're all still
    afraid

leaving his room we go for a walk   along the Coogee
    headland
wind bending grass   like a reefed handbrake
and throwing spray   into our faces
what is the Holy Spirit?   a boy with a plastic bucket and spade
asks his father   on their way back to the car
my ears strain for the answer   but the wind snatches
            it and sends it
        flying
                over the cliff face
the sea always reminds me of *La Mer*   an orchestra
of salt & movement   I imagine myself at my parents' house

playing Debussy again   on the family piano
     The Maid with the Flaxen Hair
it's afternoon   and mum's cooking dinner
in the next room   looking out the window
I can see my brother   through the backyard's fading light
knocking nails out of fence palings   whilst overhead
the jacaranda is blessing   the lawn with its flowers
each falling gently   like a final dying note

Lachlan Brown

Pictor Ignotus

(for David Malouf)

The conception is everything – grown
    from a hostile mind like a city state
in a hot wilderness. Its curve and arc.
    Two men in the beginning performed
a simple act – welding two girders
    together, then a third. A whole complex
of space – Uffizi-garish, little
    Medicis volumising over it ...

The procession of rooms – the glopping
    monitors' hum and buzz. Some primitive
Giotto's Last Supper – jungle-eyed,
    a caged figure mewling at its captors,
hook, tail, breast-mound and rude totemic line
    ("tantôt libre, tantôt rechercher") –
the miraculous Daughter of Fishes,
    fleshlipped, nightblue, shriving the horse-mackerel.

"Still glides the stream and shall forever glide."
    Five thousand miles of platitude and not
one pale god to be seen. Nolan's Burke, dead-
    eyed like some homicidal idiot,
stands sentry at the tomb of the unknown
    artist – bark and red ochre, yellow,
white, a pair of sticks tied with possum gut
    to steer through subterranean weather.

Whoever said that art doesn't conform
        to fact? A polaroid nude, the eye's un-
bridled rut blacking-out a big money
        sunset, navy yards and warm chardonnay.
Or an artefact shaped from the stolen
        inner lives of appearances. These things
like maps of impending extinction: that
        procure such insurance against themselves.

Louis Armand

Plant poem

The decision of a plant

to grow this way or that

might mimic the decision

to leave by this door or that

but ultimately like a plant

one stays put, moving only in minute,

imperceptible degrees, craning

the neck, for example, towards the sun

towards light which remains glacial

towards peace that carries spurs

towards a singular voice, a neon

strobe which may flicker or be broken

but which nonetheless shines some

small thing inwards to pinken

the discoloured mind, brighten the worsted eyes

which look this way or that

towards a door ajar but not open

extending just enough to hear as well as to feel

the work of the feet outside.

Claire Potter

Poetry of the Taliban

In *Poetry of the Taliban*, a sword beside a flower.
    Inside a narrative
on love, a stone tracks a stone across the page
    from a community
well to hospital. An unwound turban is an ex-
    tended metaphor
for a wound. A goat is a roadside device.
    A camouflaged
field-gun jumps and smokes under a hard rain
    of shell casings.
The ringtone of a phone going off beneath
    a robe sounds like
muted reports of weapons bringing down
    migratory cranes
from a dust cloud. They might have been storks
    on a day so clear
you could read into it. Perhaps the scene
    involved a crowd
of men, just returned from a mass
    beheading in the hills:
trouble with young, out-of-wedlock couples
    dancing.

Anthony Lawrence

pollen wind

the unsettled library flutters at the heart like a moth
my father who disappeared books is two years dead
I pour water from a narrow neck
at the speed of remembering dream
a dream full of my brother's only confessions
I dreamt he had been in the care of a child I didn't know I had
the pages of my notebook flick like flame

Claire Gaskin

Postcard for Marilla

The camera shutter comes down on a selection
of Cappadoccia's finest caves, as if to prove
the fact I've never been there. Whole empires
could balance upon your first tooth but this life
we have prepared for you will close more quickly
than it opens, no matter how much we love each other.

Living in a city networked by smog, I dreamed
of novellas set in Beijing where the dead
disappear into its future with each urban reinvention.
Can you distinguish reflection from light yet?
Afternoon sun catches on Mekong Delta brackish glass,
its waters thinning out up stream, one dam at a time.

One day when you are ready, I'll tell you
about great migrations we have destroyed & marsupials
you'll never meet, even as they ghost
across scrubland on the television screen. Folly
of the world's mindless plunge into convenience;
detritus accumulates across the ocean in plastic rafts.

You'll have to trust me: the index page is useless
without the body to sit before it. Afternoon: I open
the shutters on your latest sleep; overcast day slips in
& a hot westerly slaps windows in their frames
invoking another place, another time. Still-unspoken words
gather as you pull up to me on the bars of your cot.

James Stuart

P.R.B

I wish I had been painted by Millais. Maybe not as Ophelia in a tepid bath. Perhaps as Lady Macbeth. Or Titania. Or Portia. Not Brutus' Portia. Portia from *The Merchant of Venice.* I used to make you sit on a little wooden stool and pretend you were painting me. Stroke after stroke rasping against the canvas. I would unravel my strawberry plaits and stare at you. Sherry eyes. Corsage at my neck. Picking up the small crumbs of wedding cake and passing them through my gold ring. Nine times. But you still didn't get the hint. And so I am suspended in that moment. Forever bridesmaid. I can't be your Effie or your Ruskin. So blot out the canvas with grey. Euphemia's hagiography turns on a wheel and a bear, but I can't be your martyr. Writhing in my skin, I call out to Rossetti to paint me. I make you call me Guggums and cling to wild heartsease. We both know the laudanum comes later. So you paint me. Regina Cordium. Hooded lids. Heart shaped pendant. There are two still babies in the shadows. One within and one without. Broken hearted, I become your posthumous Beatrice. Dig me up Dante! Exhume me. Consume me. Shift the soil between us and gather me in your arms. Chase your journal of poems around my coffin with your fingertips as you hold me. Let me hear your mew of pleasure when you have it. At last. My copper hair fills the empty space. But the worm's hole in your journal eats away at your heart.

Cassandra Atherton

Prophecy

cliffs ahead the singing ravine
a horse gallops beside the train never tiring
who is stoking the engine? is the lion tame?
the thorn in the paw was a dream
everything ran on grease and sequins
everybody wore a smoking hand
when Habakkuk rode into the desert
with the lighter and a wafered tongue
a trail of bunting flicks and frets
like a projectionist with a stammer
there was never a bridge the horse the horse
every boom gate is a gallows
the spitfire diving for the dining car
will the yogi come out of his trance?
the jewel on his turban charging the ape
with coveting another man's wife
the ostrich's light globe head has blown
red beads across the carriage floor
a flapper girl tied to the tracks ahead
every hoof print the shape of 'you'
as the standoff continues upon the roof
three winds come clapping for hats
and it burns burns burns the ring of fire
there was never a bridge to be out

*

Habakkuk rides the wincing mule
as if it matters how you travel to your funeral
everything is melting down to murder
the mirage is a cake of trouble
the Russian who said *only blood will tell*

the sun's throwing knives never miss
may the dust he returns to catch the light
who has eaten his death cap mushrooms?
the mule knows the dangling carrot is a boot
the mule knows how things go around
how summer reacquaints us with our ugly feet
how Bertha pole dances in a caravan
animals in costumes dream of new costumes
Habakkuk rides like prophecy
his sentence dangling around his neck
rabbits knocking on wood in the cemetery
a tongue that tastes like the body of Christ
the mirage is still a cake
sometimes he hears the squeak of trees
but that must have been days ago
as somebody somewhere plays guitar
and chuckles like firewood
the bearded lady or the ringleader's wife
he should have chosen the other hand

*

it's not the storm it's the debris that kills you
in a hot chilli hallucination
eye floaters steering the eye of the film
avoid contact with the air as much as possible
people's views aside for a moment
they're calling it terminal
white goats swimming in a pool of milk
dogs nailed to the ground by thunder
the standoff continues upon the roof
and smoke in the projector's beam
how to turn away from a beautiful woman
duelling with snarls and squints
the hobbled heart and violent mind

the eagle in the baby pram
the gun he draws becomes a banana
only the lighthouse keeper knows
the extraordinary life she lives without him
if they'd only invested in spray on skin
the ape and the mushrooms come to pass
the abuse of prophecy and group hypnosis
when the only choice is how to fall
down on Habakkuk in the canyon
like a ceiling rose with a beautiful voice
about the horse about ramraid mayhem

Nathan Curnow

Rally

I marry at your feet, but only you can move me
Nu Folk dangles from a deck
My ekphrastic breastplate speaks to the abstruse courtier
Who would think I was one of fourteen?
Your Eleanor, my Isobel, whose slippers in the grate
tarry, but true empathy is kept for this

I make history in the Tower,
fleece the rent to peruse a commentary
time hovels through days' dreamt tyrant
To choir would sully this grasp
Two Americas checked off, one Ireland picked,
all these wrappings.
Hived in insignia your enchained horse canters
as entreaties whistle up a kingdom
I would push my galleons to charge for you
blowy and stern
And here I decipher some longing, the flowered verse
not sent returns to oak.
But let's walk, diplomacy can stick it
Pennants beam into air, and all trials you meant and break,
    twinned princes
not annul but stayed

Gig Ryan

Regression to the mean

A jar, a thought, a slight breeze. Who else is tired of these props
    props
and found objects? Left on their own
they form connections, attach to each other, signal new
    meanings
and while we wait in the wings for the next act to begin
for a guiding principle to wander by
we might as well reset the scene
in the cabin in the forest, perhaps, or
inevitably, return to the water, to that epitomised landscape –
the sand, the beach house, the predictable sets.

Thinking on it now, it should never have been about
what was missing from that experience
just about being there. You can't identify a problem
you're in the midst of though, and we can't go back
and do it over, even when the map is spread before us
tracing paths up through the dunes. Best not to think of
    yourself
as the driving force, as the protagonist
but more as an empty jar or a thought in the wind.

Aden Rolfe

Renovations

It was a summer of stinking heat, hell-fire days,
nothing predictable but the violence of time
whistling throu a sou' westerly, the dragon lizard
scampering to underbrush from crops of dry lawn.
Boxes in every half-filled room, masking-tape rolls,
anarchic cockroaches slewing between floorboards.
I learnt how to correct grey hair roots, presbyopia,
leaking showers. The marriage laws defied me.
Then one tradie after another, phone calls, texts.
In my alacrity, I'd confuse their names, driving
from Canada Bay to Lidcome, Ikea to Parramatta Road
for blackbutt, bamboo, terracotta. Scott from Prospect
gave a quote I accepted for all the drop sheets, all
the brawn and Epoxy sealant it took to keep me single.

Michelle Cahill

Revealed

To re-teach a thing its loveliness ...
Galway Kinnell

Nothing much lovely about Grampa Lou,
not the reek of his cigar, the ash and crumbs
tumbling from his vest as he snatched us up
onto his lap, not his prickly moustache kisses.

He'd suck his false teeth at meals, slurp soup
and slam the table in a pique, upsetting the gravy.
Made Grandma blush and squirm
with his salacious puns and Mae West jokes

and who didn't wince at his tenor trills
while listening to Sunday night opera?

He pranced like a circus bear spouting Russian,
though he was only 12 when he'd arrived at Ellis Island.
Waving his cigar, he'd brag about the two jobs he'd worked
to pay for law school at night.

Weeping was a fine art for him and while Grandma lay dying
he wailed, *Mummy, don't leave me.*
The old aunts rolled their eyes and muttered,
About time she went somewhere on her own.

At the nursing home, the staff learnt to avoid
his flirtations and the occasional pinch.
By 96, still healthy, he'd had enough
and refused to eat.

Cocooned in white blankets, he was
a shrivelled balloon minus his bluster and puff.
Groaning in his sleep, wrestling with bedclothes,
with beckoning angels, he'd cry out, *No! No!*
raising his palm to ward them off.

His eyelids flickered, then snapped open.
What time is it?
One pm, Grampa.
Seeing me, recognition dawned.
He asked after my children, recalling ages and names,
then drifted off only to wake and demand,
What time is it?

Once he sat straight up, grasping my hands in his icy ones.
He leaned his grizzled cheeks close.
Eyes, brimming like Russian lakes, revealed

the tender boy
he'd so skilfully concealed
beneath overcoats of bravado.
A luminous boy, we'd never met.

In the light of that naked gaze, he whispered,
You are beautiful!
spoken to me and to the reflection
of that boy beaming back.

The bare room glowed and everything
all of it – was made lovely.

Laura Jan Shore

Revisiting Yugoslavia: *Rijeka, Croatia*

I don't know why but I often think
I was born in my father's city, Trieste,

(the statues of Joyce, Saba and Svevo
stand in footpaths where they once
walked and thought)

and not in Rijeka,
in a country that doesn't exist anymore.

My cousin's son points to a canal
lined with small coloured boats,
and my confusion surfaces.
I stare at it
the old border with Italy.

Rijeka's language I've forgotten how to speak.
I speak my father's tongue.
I remember my mother's words:
You know how much your father hated the Communists.

I don't know if it's mine or someone else's
but a deep sadness smears the gaps of the hours.
I imagine my father's days.
They become part of me:
the contempt for the country
that took his country
is the unease,
the shame,
I feel for my birthplace.

Rosanna Licari

Rise and Shine

'What is a / poem, anyway . . .'
                    —James Schuyler

Morning's kiss
            your kiss
                    leaves and noisy sparrows—

        outside
                the open window
                        guys are up to something
                                        of importance—

            '... the sewer's not ...

                        can you get
                                the fucking waders ...'

Cameron Lowe

Rupert in Japan

Prince Shotoku, who dedicated the temple at Horyuji,
the moment he was born leapt up to pray
fourteen centuries ago and quite unlike our Rupert
who was six weeks till his first smile.

We stare at the deer. Now in Nara Prefecture
eight months older, in temples of shopping
and mountain air, his gestures much closer to thought.
Existing in a state no one's ever known.

My book's page. Its black ink.
And it's not quite prayer.
More like paper's feel
of the words.
And a bell resounds.

Paul Magee

Season's Greetings

Digital breathalyser portable garden trolley
crying kitten weight management capsules
gesso moulded cup plinth faux drawers
no photo fruit motif pineapple berries

Lap desk brass inlaid corners opening
fitted mahogany interior blue tooled leather
surface breaks to pen rest antler ink well
gilt Arabic numerals silvered dial

Revolutionary subjects in profile 1680s
gold edge porcelain birds breaks and losses
pastel *portrait presume* provenance verso
paper scales alcohol thermometer storm glass

Kate Lilley

Self Portrait at 65

i.m. Quinton Duffy 13.11.1971–10.9.2005

I
I sit alone watching a Japanese anime film
on a large screen.
A moth flickers across projected light.

II
I've been trying to write about a death,
my grand daughter's father, aged thirty-three,
a perfect human being
who loved Japanese anime films.
Past midnight in a hospital ward
my daughter kisses his inert head
while her mother and I look on.

III
There was a "famous" incident in his childhood.
His mother hears him, aged five,
chattering to his one week old sister,
asking questions.
He appears crestfallen in the kitchen doorway:
"That baby doesn't seem to like me.
She won't talk."

IV
My daughter's regret – and she laughs –
he missed the fifth season
of *The Sopranos*,
The Brothers Karamazov
is buried with him, unfinished,

his shirt sleeves as he liked them
partly rolled up.

V
The females of the household
(my wife and daughter) resolve
Ada, not yet three, and I
will shower together –
"a male presence."

VI
Three weeks after Q's death I fly down to Julia.
She wakes me after midnight.
We drive the old brown Volvo to the hospital,
the same car as three weeks earlier.
It feels like the same journey
as a small child struggles for breath.
By three a.m., after antihistamines,
Ada's pedalling a plastic car
across vinyl tiles
in the fluorescent calm of Emergency.
There are lurid flowers planted on the wall.

VII
I read about an improbable event:
one of the archaea
that light up marshes at night
fused with an oxygen eating bacterium
and became us,
all complex life,
and the improbable fungus
too small for hospital microscopes
that killed Q as he lay in an isolation ward.

VIII

It's six months since Q's death.
I sit in a glass room typing letters
for a research foundation.
The garden wilts in the sun,
overgrown with climbing roses.
Tomorrow I stay with my daughter
who carries his unborn child.

As the sun declines I switch off my screen –
I've an hour to mow the lawns.
I change into a torn t-shirt
and faded trousers
ripped with splashes of white paint and yellow chlorine.
My mower starts with one pull –
a surprise – but now it can't stop
until the petrol runs out
or I jerk the lead from the spark-plug.
Its staccato roar consumes the grass on my driveway.
In the street a young man
is packing his young family into a car.
They hurry to close the doors,
alarmed by this obsessive old man,
red-faced and sweating in his clouds of dust,
as I reach the grass on the verge
and mow beside their car.
The blades are spitting out topsoil fines and dead leaves.
A pebble ricochets.
On the opposite footpath an Asian girl
holds a handkerchief to her nose.

The young man parks down the road and is back,
mild-mannered, fair hair and egg-shaped head.
I depress the throttle to hear his reproach:
"You could at least have waited!"

"I was embarrassed," I say,
"I do the lawns in a particular order
and I've a tennis court to mow before it's dark."
He nods and walks away.

IX
My postscript, aged 68.
Julia telephones
and reads a poem of nineteen syllables.
She asks how many syllables for a haiku.
"Seventeen," I reply.

She'll send the corrected haiku
as a text message:
"and you can put it in a poem –
So it will be preserved."

This is Julia Lehmann's haiku,
(now a syllable short):
"Widowed 4 years, I find
the wig you made from your hair,
(still scented)."

X
A postscript to the postscript:
I have to set up the camera again
with my self portrait
for a final tracking shot.
I'm 69
and having radiotherapy.
Lying on the slab
surrounded by lights
in an empty room with pop music playing
I shut my eyes
so I don't panic.

That night my daughter
texts me another haiku for Q
(the number of syllables correct):
"Always fluorescent
in the room where you died,
my howl is a ghost there."

Geoffrey Lehmann

from Shaping the Dark: Three Readings of Tony Lloyd's Oil on Linen Painting 'On a Dark Night You Can See Forever'

ii. Night holds history inside its black cape.
You know when your unit reaches the top of this ridge
your truck will turn, unload, and the firing begins.
Sarajevo sits sparkling, a diamond sunk below the ring of hills;
cosmopolitan, blended Ottoman and Austrian and Bosnian,
a jangle of colour and bright spirit, a tight woven history.
You enjoy the lights now; 'like fairyland', your mother used to say;
and she'd wonder: 'what are you doing here?'
People below don't know what you know.
That they are now targets, ducks in a shooting gallery.
That fifteen hundred children will be killed, ten thousand adults;
three hundred mortars a day will burn their books, crush their
     history,
buildings and bodies fragmented.
For four years – no heat, no power, no water, no food.
Then they will know blackness:
a lightless city where only your flares will ignite it
so mortars can find victims in the dark.
That long black road may go on forever.

Robyn Rowland

snowy

they flash past
like cyclists through
red lights with or without
consequence is there a need
to hurry is there an agenda
as they wait for particle
rearrangement, reassignment
another incarnation; do they
get impatient or is this messing
around merely spirit at play, a
version of 'being' italicised; are
the dead on the look out for
groceries, hungry as they visit
dreams footpaths crevices
vestibules auditory canals, beings
we recognise, or don't; what
fills the space between the 'be'
and the 'ing', what would coleridge
have to say in his lime-tree bower;
you surprised me deep in slumber
under the snowy doona, your
emerald dress like a sudden
summer –

Joanne Burns

Soar

It began with structural analysis of a dragonfly wing.
The first task was to create
flow in the DelFly II.
Wing flexibility in 'clap-and-fling'
and 'clap-and-peel' were tested.
But what of appearance variation cues
and obstacle avoidance?
In the end they took a sky segmentation approach,
while others dealt with complex tail effects
in flapping flight. Even so, after years of work,
hear-and-avoid problems beset
indoor and outdoor dragonflies.
All parties were insisting on micro air vehicles
quieter than any insect that ever hovered
over a lake ('water source').
One bright spark solved it,
You want quiet? I'll give you guys quiet, he said.
This is gunna be the quietest bug on the planet,
quieter than anything we've done before;
quieter than any soft-spoken woman at a well
shielding her eyes from the glare,
from dreams of water
in the insectless heat of high summer.

A. Frances Johnson

Sorrowful

The house is up for tender and will be sold.
Houses always sell – in the end. Even if it is
for the land. Smoking out or treading down
the haunts takes three days, or even longer.

A child always has a father even if the child
must learn to forgive that father for almost
everything. A father is just a man, just one
more member of our clan, one of our skin.

And the mother, a roomy doorway, a pathway,
a vivid gash – making the baby up as she goes
along. If she holds the little one too close to her
it will have to kick hard to make her let it go.

The brother and the sister and the cousin keep
all the secrets of how you used to be. Oh a long
long time ago. In the meeting place impossible
to prevent the family smell from burgeoning.

The tea slops into the saucer, the wine is opened
and poured into that glass of memories, that gift
that was given to a dead woman, before she died.
Some of us drink tea, and some of us drink wine.

The house will be sold, the broken window was
repaired a long long time ago, some of us will
die soon – some of us will turn over in our beds
and do what is needful to call the new one home.

Jennifer Compton

Spiritual

A place of crosses and bullet shells
sold by auction. Flattened cars

sold by negotiation. Muddy ribcage

to be inspected by appointment
with an undead agent. Vendors

stinking cadavers. Property
of decomposition. A house amazing

-ly decrepit. Did we enjoy prosperity
's graveyard? To report

conditions of infestations? No

place like home. It's me and you

dusting this debris, kicking vultures
out of our craters. Floor boards

become of coffins, curtains
of bloody uniforms. Let's haunt this house.

Ali Alizadeh

from Stages of Balthazar (with a Chorus of Elders)

1.

Uncertain grey of early morning,
a quick warm cataract
is the birth of donkey,
now stuck with grass and its mother's gum, legs bunched
under like unlit kindling

The field totters and rights itself
as the foal stands planted fast,
lapidarian beside a sun that shakes
in its haze, an earth
shirking underfoot

> —beautiful he
> stirs up still things

Trailing afterbirth regally
the mother-mountain instead comes to him:
strikes him over the head with
a teat to set
his flesh on its parting way

> —be ahead of all partings,
> as long gone already
> like winter in spring;
> and be ever-dying in your chosen-poison;
> the cut-glass cup that shatters itself
> and resounds down the great diminishing;
> be—yet know
> of its antipode,

nothing-source of your trembling ontology:
Oh I am here! And as such
I assent!

Great love overshoots its end
and shifts back its conception:
Was it then a thin
girl hand reached down to touch his curly brow
commanding in a tiny-headed tremolo
Father let us have him.

—Only know:
this is the animal that never was.
Of course he wasn't.
But as we gave him space
the poor pure beast persisted
and in this place so white unfenced
he barely needed to exist yet raised his head

L. K. Holt

Strange, unremarkably so

They just want to keep talking when I read a normal poem,
but an experimental sound poem
brings a whole bar of drunks to silence.

Loading up the car, I admire the enhanced reflections of scudded
clouds on the back window, the sun a bright disc.
Hey, you could watch a solar eclipse on this thing!

The bathroom mirror says I can leave the house looking pretty good,
but when I see my reflection in shop windows I want to go home.

Completing an unremarkable transaction on the phone, the customer
says 'love you' and hangs up.

On the freeway, it's best not to think about the possibility of dying.
Try to marvel at how cooperative we can be.

Peak hour, I notice a puff of white fluff from the car in front. Then
another. Then a burst of white feathers. A perfect white dove falls
plop! onto the road in front of my car, sits up, flies away. I think, the
driver of that car is a magician, or maybe an escape artist.

Tonight, I was greeted by the neighbour's cat on the back verandah.
Proof that when a cat dies, all the other cats redistribute themselves
to fill the empty space.

Anna Fern

Street Encounter

Napier St., late morning
a blonde woman gets out of a Yellow Cab, pulls the rose
out of her hair, and throws it in the gutter
        outside her house.

The old woman
with arthritis gets to the Hoddle St. bus (outside
the Flats); she still knows
        how to laugh.

        HUNGRY JACKS --- empty.

Small shot / Big Night: Ad for alcohol at the Bus stop

        A Vietnamese woman gets out of the bus

        : H â T

H_2O is the name of a Hand Car Wash.

CALL THIS CUNT 0423451499

        ENCORE --- will bring you pizza.

        Ad: Red Meat: the Home of Quality

        The Workers (on
the footpath) are excavating; pipe on shoulder ========
        And piping the whole of the street.

        A woman walking 2 dogs.
Cross over; – Which way? ------ untangles the leash!

CALL 0423451499 4 FREE HEADJOB

*! BangerS & Mash, peas $8.

A kid on the footpath (outside

the café) with red boots on, is jumping on all the puddles;

checking-out how

deep

they are.

A woman walking along
the footpath, is draped in the Australian Flag. (On her way
to the Sports ground, i guess). A red rose
in her hair.

An entrance (to a Brothel) called Ladies + Gentlemen's.
A pretty woman outside.
....
(Not related).

Over the Hoddle St. Bridge (up
the hill) and everyone's)))))))))))))) on bicycles.

The YEAH MAAN RASTA
RAUNT looks very tired; Could do with a good paint job.

Draagon stops me (on
the corner). What you doing? he sez. I tell him
i'm going up the street here, to kill a man, shoot-Up,
run around the block, walk pass some Bouncers,
smile at a Copper, slap a PUNK about,

go back to Vincent's, and pretend
        nothin' happened.
He sez, why don't i come round later, and
        have a choof.

π.O.

from Succession

(iii)

Maybe I should have held onto it longer.
I did my best thinking in the dairy.
All those years of dipping hands in hot water,
feeding calves, ploughing on Sundays, chasing pigs.
Now I'm chasing what's left of this life –
these days I don't even buy green bananas.
Wouldn't it be great to do it all again?
Start off with nothing, go into debt, shift a bit
of country. Farmers have hung themselves for less.
I drive the ute over every inch of grass remembering
afternoons turning in the seat, face into dust, checking
the discs, rocks weighing them down, the back
out of joint, bone rubbing on bone. If I didn't hand it over
he would have left. Some days I get silly notions in my head.

Brendan Ryan

Summer

Summer. The coach veers to a screeching halt. Divided into
    two groups, women and men.
I soon would wake up among the infirm.
Molded. A modicum of light.

What hits me then, a sudden
Your face
and 'Never', a curl of a sound
and all these years, my whole life end-to-end.

In the grand run-down house, they give me a small cabin
which looks like a single room once taken by Van Gogh
minus the writing desk
The caretaker says he's Manichean, and will be kind

He hands me a Napoleonic washbowl
Indecipherable years scratched out at the base, saying
Use
For the snow.

Nguyen Tien Hoang

The Bat Corridor

Or we could leave the house, the pressure
of its walls and light, its hard words
bumbling against the windows,
and go down to the gully where the creek-bank
collapses with the autumn rains, something
you could fall for and put your lips to.
Come on, bring the mattock for the thistles;
hold it between us if you wish.

We won't know what makes them
unwrap the bandaged thumbs of their bodies
and bear away from the canopy
the moment the day's balance tips towards night;
we won't decipher their insect-seeking sonar,
or tally the number of beetles they catch
and the number they miss.
Yet these little crepuscular bats,
flying by hand, led by their petalled noses,
have us mesmerised in the spiky pea,
motionless, transported.

Scouts sent ahead of the night, detachments
from dark like escaped pocket linings,
one is suddenly there, a sharp dip and yaw
over the paddock, then gone; there
and gone, a relay of presence and absence.
They are mystery and guesswork;
their flickering fly-past in the half-light is enough
to make us question the worth of seeing clearly
and settle for partial blindness; enough,
when it's time to go in, to make you
shift the mattock to the other hand.

Louise Oxley

The break

To prevent tragedy the brush must be cut an angles,
no less than ten metres between squares.

Here my ancestors planted the buffalo grass
where it burns too hot for the native plants to seed

and we need these squares between land
to stop it sparking all the way to our homes.

After her third institutionalization they suggested
that perhaps my Aunt's cingulated cortex be severed,

there was too much leaping between lobes.
Now I am the oldest member of my father's family

not to have undergone inpatient treatment
for whatever fire caused my grandmother's suicide

and the beating my grandfather gave which sparked it.
I try to hold my line. To be the space

large enough to let it all burn out.
But out of my native climate I arc and arc.

Caitlin Maling

The Brooklyn International Motel

Oily light in the corridors
and the smell of old suitcases
we borrowed from your parents.

You write our room number
on the back of your hand, spread
postcards on rough carpet.

Through the louvers
we watch emergency lights flash,
dragging cars out of fog.

Later, in the dark, you search for the bed.
Crookedness
meets your fingertips.

You grip my bent leg
like a branch
to climb up and sit on.

In other rooms,
people wait for hot water with a hand
in the shower.

From these windows
the world looks nothing like itself.
The ceiling has stolen some low stars.

Come closer.
The slow roll of cities
will turn us home soon.

Across the Pacific
the battered poinciana still stands
outside the house we live in.

Ella Jeffery

The Conscience of Avimael Guzman

All Peruvians are liars – Mario Vargas Llosa
Peru is not a novel – Shining Path graffiti

In grey wind where snow turns to ice, leaving no shelter,
you are murdering the woman who made you feel guilty,
who called you a *fascisti*. Your fingers at her throat
you examine her pores and her pock-marks,
her teeth broken by a rifle butt
because her parents worshipped an icon of Stalin.
A high fog is breaking in the acquiescent village.
Faces carved from the hard material of nature
reveal no motives. Your hands close on nothing:
wood, weeds or water. Impossible to tell
if these people are servants to force alone
or to your foreign currency of words
translated from another language – the promise
of conquest, the repossession of forgotten land.
Your eyes fix on the face of the woman,
her ideas reduced to manageable flesh and bone.
What else could subdue them but your own
nervous retraction, making a virtue of fear.
Your tongue removing itself into black cavities,
your eyes concealed among Indians, watching
the woman's body slowly digested by insects.
The strings of your nerves drawn shrill
by the need to maintain a single extreme moment,
but that was an error, a point of mathematics:
better to proceed by denial, eating your own words
compacted and swallowed in gutters.
The fabricated voice of the journals dissolves behind you,
Your carefully bound diaries left on a train
now somewhere in a distant country – maybe Russia,

the terminus, the last exit. The veins in your cheeks
crackle red, and you are outside time, awaiting
the moment of ignition. But these are autumn colours,
half-formed mountains at the edge of the world.
The Amazon running to rock. Vast crowds
milling together, resisting the pressure to meld or mesh.
At first there was anger, in the fluttering walls of the throat,
at the sight of those faces barely released from stone,
brown feet roasted over open fires.
Torturers winding back their watches
at the sign of the scar, at the hour of the sentry.
Americans with flaccid hands. The light like shroud-cloth
burning your skin. You made yourself dark,
withdrawing into the shadows of the century, accepting nothing.
You are speaking to yourself thanks to the magic
of an alien technology, which is your own,
or at least helps you belong to your time.
But how it really happens, how the same words recur
in this haphazard way outside of any system
remains a mystery. A voice speaking over the radio
mirrors your own, and you cannot break the habit
of these reflections, cannot even retrace your steps.
An insidious machine is reading your thoughts.
The woman raises her head grotesquely,
and even though you are immersed in shiny blood
there is nothing left to be offered or consumed.
The magic of cheap rhetoric is retained
like a forgotten taste, brushing your tongue.
All the things that you can touch refer to secrecy
or symbols, but is that magic any more than a good card-hand
or a huge library reverberating messages between lines of shelves?
You fear asking the simplest question
because the answer is always the same,
and the voice that returns it is the familiar dominating one –
your teacher, your master, robbing you of all will,

keeping you as a servant.
The desire to subvert yourself, to speak
in the voice of another, to knock a chaos
into this order of illusions. And when they pass over you,
these shadows distinct as faces piercing the surface of water,
what do they drag in their wake? The presidential candidate's
dream-speech delivered in bubbles of his own blood.
The desire to destroy. A selection of words
to mask your jealousy, every tentative emotion concealed.
Your arrogance the revolver in its holster.
Because there is no longer any guilty internal world,
your private thoughts lead you to a plain
where huge figures stand frozen, towers and monuments
shuttling messages into the air, light patterns
and gaudy over-obvious symbols.
There are no more images for you to touch,
only these hard prints on the eye
mistaking jungle-foliage for military uniforms.
Extinction breathes its gentle colours,
pastels of tensions released. Falling softly into a chair
you believe you are outside everything,
a light tune disappearing. At last
you become leader, compelled to speak.
But there is danger, for what have you left to confess
except constructions? The high chair, the fabricated podium,
disgust you like some story spilled at gunpoint.
You take the woman into your arms, but dark smoke
has entered your bones, and there is no remedy
but the need to continue travelling among these tortured bodies,
these trees, these flayed mountains.
You wanted to capture precision,
the insides of things, but each new word
dazzles you, is a prism of caught light,
and you are frozen in captivation.
Each second snaps like a forced door.

You have been absent from the city too long,
concealed in an ambush of riddles,
and now you are scarcely recognisable.
The clear strategies inhaled at high altitudes,
formed from clear air, are swept clean away
by your embarrassing forgetfulness.
What was the use of all the lost time
learning that you could no longer lie?
Perhaps you were only parroting
the words of a saviour, practical solutions
that carry across the seaboard
like the sound of distant gunfire.
The demagogue's beard cultivated in a garbage dump.
The priest's sash sweeping across polished boards
as prickly infection wipes a baby's mouth.
You are too malleable. A servant's hysteria
scours you with painful laughter. Lawless
your shining objects shake from the walls.
Make neat piles of them. Scrub your empty face
until it burns. Make up a story.

John Hawke

The Dark Sisters

for Stephen Edgar and Judy Beveridge

If it's possible
as you travel
you should turn north and see Glencoe.
Some will say no—
keep a sense
of the Renaissance
about you. I know that you are not among those
who choose
to ignore what history's shown us to be,
beneath a grandeur or grandiosity.
Be sure to go
late of a long afternoon (although
it is dark there in the blaze of noon).
The tourist buses have moved on
at that hour
when you arrive by bike or car;
and as you stand alone
in the ravine
you will experience the Sublime,
which Burke defined
as Nature that is 'terrible'
(but which enlivens, if the watcher is safe for a while).
Hard to tell
the lie of the land—
those three long ridges incline, each to its mound
that is a misshapen, bloated globule
in a swamp, or on murky sump-oil.
The hills are stolid,
a cold lava, stone-naked,
or they can appear

to rear
at the angle
of a bull seal
when it plunges ashore.
There is a constantly seeping water
that is silver,
striated on each billowing slope.
What I want to evoke
is the summer—how it seems to have let fall a sodden cloak.
In winter, there hove
closely above,
from out of murk,
the Flying Dutchman's hulk,
but with April, a stream is gibbering its way
in the floor of the valley.
Such a place
was like a man who had a 'gallows face',
of whom they'd have said
he invited
his involvement in tragedy.
The light at the time I say
is on the loins
of these stocky mountains,
like the sword blade they would clean
beneath the arm, on their linen,
but not on plaid,
and carried lowered.
The MacDonald clan was hospitable
to a rabble
in the pit of winter,
1692, as required by honour.
At their hamlet of whitewashed stone,
through the vale, they'd taken in
each steaming cow and pig and hen,
and the 129

mercenaries, who outnumbered them,
come to proclaim
William as king, imposed upon
Scotland, too. The chieftain
had been loath
or tardy about the oath,
who lay down
with arthritis and chilblain,
and now must pay a fine.
The interlopers sprawled
along the bench, in each household,
watching the children fed from a spoon,
and drank the whisky, with its fume
like the mist above a loch.
What a piece of work
is man—how devious
in the spontaneous
refined high level
of his devilishness.
Not one of the troop betrayed its intent;
and nothing was meant
for the hosts, on turning up
a card. They noticed only the hearth fire leap
in a drowsy pupil.
Ten days passed (an ordeal
of itself) before the signal
at dawn—a bonfire, in which the families woke
and saw how murder broke
out of those faces. A sword went in
the servant girl, where the soldiers had lain.
The stranded or fleeing were chopped down—
they shed a limb
as they tried to climb
on the salt-packed snow,
or saw a sword-tip throw

about them the watery
loop of blood. Blood flew away
like the flight of the galaxy.
Some were allowed
to escape, who'd have to wade
thigh-deep, with just a shawl—
like broken crows they crawled, their call
flapping. When you come into this region
you won't need to summon
what you should feel—
our old disquiet, of betrayal,
will overwhelm. I have thought
on what is meant
by the dark sisters, those immemorial
mourners, in their veil.
Whatever level
of existence, however deep we plumb,
things come
in packages, are separate;
they co-operate, or assert
themselves, to annihilate
what constricts them. All things, we find, will fluctuate
on this scale. It is said the truth can set us free,
if only of the illusory.—
When you are there, you might feel
that evil is in the molecule.

Robert Gray

the dead are with us

the dead stand by us
peer over our shoulders
into the coffin
for this long last glimpse
no glass
just this final mirror
there's always
one hair out of place
and poignant that
they cannot touch

you read it here

the dead speak
in the eternal present
that's how it is when
your date's set in stone
on the far side
of a hyphen

Kit Kelen

The Ear Especially

You don't need eschatology to see the finitude
in all this. Cantilever arm of all sweetness,
pinions of every description
in the sinew of its reaching out. And towards
what? The globe is fine corpulence, the flesh
of the ear especially,

vigour of sports car on wet May bitumen slighting
the bone catacomb smart. Paris, hello. Where
have you hidden my brother, and Now,
my brother's brotherhood. There is a Southern Californian
song about all of this that eschatology
cannot penetrate. So stop, sweet claw of new day,
digits clammy.

The clay pits, to gasp with hand on back of head,
to be lulled to sleep like the puppet infanta,
side with brother clover and fatten wanton,
lope the lambent disguise if but only in the moment
of finitude. Need not finitude to see the sweetness
in all of this that made eschatologies
unrenewable, when instead,

and we do know this, the fossil only comes twice,
as in: all time under, the all time no time above.
That grasp, darling hand, park your car, knowing restlessness
and velocity in the woken, in the face.

Corey Wakeling

The God of Bone and Antler

What passes here for air is dry.
Four bare rooms and four doorless frames
sixteen unwindowed walls of caulked pine
and countless things with claws that scrabble
in the dry above.
If it lives
it lives like a shadow, preceding and anterior
to the light, tethered at the edge of vision.
Your feet below are naked.
As you creep across the boards
there is a scraping, a thunk
a hiss, clock, hiss and clock
of limbs as they strike ancient wood.
An antiphony of bones, a twitching cow skull
in a nest of horns.
It has no songs, it is kin to stone and ferryman to beasts;
language makes no purchase
and keeps no token or effect.
You wonder as you go within
elbows held over your breast
if it thinks like a draught horse working a bit –
teeth wearing flat on steel.
If it lives, it is behind,
cracked hoof seeking the shelving of your heart.

Daniel East

The inevitable beauty of the viewer when faced with the partitionist tactics of the situationist lover

You and your beauty ask questions of the viewer such as
What is Form   and   Why is this Happening?
The viewer not wanting to exceed the beauty
of the inoperable sees she must match its unstoppable
theory to overdue notions of the apartheid of literature.
Nothing to see in the spectacle of your lips
but the insistence of the letter in the mire of
situationist abandonment. Keep telling yourself that
the poem is a container for the formless horror of your
eyes as emotion skinning you to the scrutiny of the
automaton as inadequate representation of the poem as a
container for the formless horror of the delimited passion
of the never stops not being written

Fiona Hile

The Life Inside

A little house, a little house.
Heard from the yard:
fresh voices at the door.
A little house.

A little house.
The shelves that fill,
and cups along the board.

A little house.
Two chairs pushed close,
the crossword page filled out.

A little house.
Heard from the bed:
the hot wind all night long.

A little house.
The photos stare.
The phone shrills once and stops.

A little house.
Heard by no ear
the messages repeat.
A little house.

Judith Rodriguez

The orchard

Happiness came with such a vengeance ...
In the darkness, an apple
Had left its branch
'Last night, whose heart thumped violently?'
Someone fainted in the thunderous rain
A fine shadow
Swept the land before it died

– the orchard in the summer, shining light spots
Were following me all the time
Under a tree, I listened, my ears pricked
Within the clean flesh of the fruit, a creek rushed scouring
I sensed that happiness was slow
And that it required me to lighten my steps

Branches extending themselves, the green waves of the orchard
    were quietly rolling
It was not till then that the old orchard peasant told me
That he sometimes would dream of his own death, like an
    apple falling

Hu Xian (translated by Ouyang Yu)

The owl painting

The owl looks angry. It also, I think, looks very frightened.
The artist has been scrupulous. The beak
And claws are not to be trifled with.

The setting is specific – a Queensland bathroom
Already old-fashioned if not dilapidated
So that the bird, perched on the rim, looks out of place.

That is the idea: discomfort and confusion
Enough for anger to rise in anyone. It does.
So that the painting expresses complete resentment.

Why my former wife bought it is completely obvious
and it has nothing to do with value – at least, not as money.
It has something to do with isolation, however.

And, for the first time, I think of that bathroom
As place of confinement, a tortuous space.
Wings are not given to us, but claws are.

There is nothing more terrible than confinement
Or more endangering and threatening than fear.
We might not have beaks but we have other weapons.

Thomas Shapcott

The Roadside Bramble

Walking late by a roadside bramble
Hoops of brittle thorn, a caul of dead grass, quiet rust
Frost-burnt une feuille serrate
Motes fall and swirl as brassy notes and cobwebs
Tangle straw stems in mossy dirt, the gravel wash
A stripped page of newspaper rotting, crushed
Polyethylene terephthalate
Half-full of piss or rain water, the sign of a dog
Chalk eroded in the furrow of a wheel
Gone a little wide on the corner, or a near miss
Now overgrown in parochial paspalum, afternoon light
Cold and real, bees somewhere in the shadows
A thought of honey in the thicket
The grey common behind a wire fence half down in the damp
Bruise hung on the smoke
Of a sundog burnt in hazy sky, translucent
Sleep stuck in the cavernous dawn of a bramble there by the roadside
Where I hurry into the emaciated past
Where dry straw recedes speechless into the middle distance
A skein of mist settling over a paddock
Air still, damp, muddy in my nose as the scent of blood
Steel cold hockey bone blue, knee high
Twigs and the hair on my skin lift in the golden aperture
Of the sky's milk crystal
Fanned behind a brittle stand of eight grey poplars
Pines melting in the middle distance
Dark green glass shards sliding into the earth
A path trodden flakes of rock
Through clumps and bristles of grass and wet-stemmed seed-heads
Dropping over bright plastic bits and rusting caps
Squashed with dirt into a bleak loam
A field scattered with the bones of my predecessors

Wandering aimlessly over turquoise hills, smoky dead trees
I find I'm outside the future, overgrown
Great walls of roots & earth crumbling sodden in the muddy weather
Wooden claws of hackberry gum
Knotted foetal in the grey wind, contrail chords in the sky
Lines unfurling between hard matter and blue
Blown above a jetliner's silver precipice
Disappearing into the end of a broken branch
Time and space are orange as mud in gravel
Trees a-glint with a wild fire
Sparks flying across the horizon the singular grey abyss
Every bramble has been the same, I think
As they all rush from my past like black swans, snow geese
Drawn into the circle of gravel
A formation of birds dropping suddenly into mind
As I walk around, feathers widening
Angular as they land into the poverty of the world
The horizon always looking, then retreating from the present
And all it holds, the skeletal frame of a sparrow chick
Its absent eye resting on a quartz pebble
Left as a sign to the logic of inhuman death, clear, immensely old
A grain of cold stone, the indifferent raw tangle
In a bracken fern halo, the silent forehead of a sickle moon
Tacked strangely to a wooden light-pole
The sound of water tinkling and gurgling, treble & bass
A silver banner fluttering and wending
Through the poplars and brace of pines
Darkness somehow equal to its bright and random melody
Caught in the cold pomegranate at the road's end
Crimson flesh held in a world of white foam
Mist correlates, transpires, solid shapes beneath the moon
& stars, hips and haws, love and hate
No matter how opaque and powerless I become
I still cry into the night as it springs burning into felony
Emptiness glowing through dry yellow stalks

No match for the whorl at the crown of your head
Telescoped to a galaxy, a whale from the old world bare
As a chunky key-ring nob lost in the mossy grit
Where I walk & look, no doubt within
Perhaps hell-bent as gravel paths spread from me chaotically
All the same, having wandered here before
And knowing how each will always yield its own
I fall away into the roadside ditch
Sticks and mud stuck in my hair, the back of my throat
Catching the gold sunset
Behind, of course, bitumen spread Bauhaus thin and black
A wall of glass windows over the road
A mercury pool shimmering in the wind
The whole reflected world shuddering.

Peter Minter

The Slide

Sometimes they put you in seas
or rivers without telling you.
The river is dark, let's say
and trees are low over you.
In the branches are owls
making noises like a machine
breathing.

After you come away from this
you have a scar and a jar
where you swim.
It is chemical, archaeological
and violent.

So you wash it all away.
It's too early for things to be
broken or twisted
but even when you run, you fall.

All your life, if you could fly
all your life slides from under you
and you do not have to swallow
water or hear it.

You do not have to but you must
as the clouds fall without telling you.

Jill Jones

from The Vanity of Australian Wishes

8

One Saturday evening Forbes and I leave his monastic,
lino-paved North Carlton house, heading for Brunswick Street.
We know what to expect:
Bohemia as a free-market, tolerant-enough, rock'n'roll
republic for the Kids in Black, though tonight
hosting the Templestowe hordes,
the Menai, MacGregor and Joondoolup hordes
who John observes, 'Go for all this
with the same intensity they'd go for wowserism.'
Admirably correct of course, and I won't forget it,
but does he feel as if some Leagues Club
propped by the four pillars of its demos ethos
Good beer, good tucker, good mates, good times
might somehow be wowser-free and purer?
I dare not ask him.
                    Meanwhile, one or two ks west
The Great Gangitano is doubtless shaking down,
or planning shaking down, or celebrating shaking down
the subjects of his lulu kingdom. Then later,
with Jason and whoever needs the thrill-enough,
find him in King Street, lots of heads in King Street,
some to get cracked, some to look away;
lots of tits too, sweet and getting sweeter;
and lots of space to be caught on camera just like that,
like that all-too-real-thing, a movie star, is meant to be.
What this man needs is a brother, to set his limits,
for if you must standover, please … with style?
Broadsheet, tabloid or talk, whatever gives a crew its name
they have to deserve their reputation and Alphonse
you just aren't deserving it.

Is this what made them visit you
that mid-summer Friday night?
It might've been when the bro-talk started, it sure was where
and when it stopped: lots of shouting in a big house.
Know the it of You're losing it?
Well you lose plenty but when the it occurs,
your mate Jason loses plenty more
and the Robert De Niro of Lygon Street
finishes as the Joe Pesci of Templestowe,
whacked from behind because he was a fucking lulu.
         The following evening I visit John who leaves
for an hour, push-biking in the heat,
probably to Preston for his cough mixture
(whatever that mixture's holding in reserve
spirits are resurrected, though little else could be).
All doors and windows of a stuffy house
opening onto a stuffy Melbourne,
we watched The Merchant of Venice,
a series of static tableaux perhaps, though
drenched in poetry, with John like some De La Salle brother
quizzing boys on certain passages, characters
and all its ambiguity.
                        I'll speak to him once more,
we'll talk about Bruce Dawe, how he writes 'themes',
how English teachers love their 'themes',
how because of 'themes' Bruce Dawe makes the syllabi,
how his books sell and how, if not rich
he's far richer than we're becoming,
though which one day could still be ours
like Shakespeare might be. Yes.
      And then the wish-list ends.
And then the day they're burying that other one
John dies.

Alan Wearne

The View from GOMA

I can see into the empty offices
and on the far bank, through archways,
a factory yard frames groves
of plastic crates stacked onto pallets,
where trucks jackknife
to reverse park.

It's quiet here between shows. The river
side hotel advertises cable tv,
empty balconies (a single chair
and aircon units) level with the traffic.
Clouds are building. Through a break
XXXX.

Observe: a sign flashes, a man walks
across to the hostels on Roma.
Thunder is in the air, it's time
-lapse, incremental, and no-one
lifts their heads, as cars exit
the bridge to approach the roundabout.

I address the park – soft-headed
with grasses, formal with bike paths,
where only water-pipes and stop-cocks
lie prone on the grass.

Angela Gardner

The ward is new

A signature and so
I'm through two doors and in
this freshly opened smallish airport

terminal of light
which slants in through clerestories,
a view out to the mountains.

The whole thing's done with courtyards,
a scattering of smokers,
thoughtful mostly, sometimes talking

softly to themselves.
Mainly it's communal,
a wary sort of wit.

A Psychiatric Treatment Order
is what my friend has got:
medications, calibrations,

side effects to be withstood,
a restoration, mil by mil.
The rooms are pleasantly *en suite*,

a motel minus cars.
The staff are friendly, well intentioned,
gentle with their skills

and on the other side of glass.
The patients wave to catch their eye,
dance perhaps or shout a little.

The afternoon is turning drowsy.
The brain's electro-chemical,
sparking its connections.

What are we but its tuning really?
In three weeks time, or maybe months,
his friends and he will reacquire

a tightrope-walker's balance.
They'll be a present to themselves.
It's all approximate, they know:

the tentative nomenclatures,
the rescue wrought by measurement,
the let's try this, the let's try that.

The talking cure is later on
and soft around the edges,
the childhoods now too far away

and slipping into fiction –
or narrowed to the past few weeks:
the shoebox of a family;

the square dance of addiction.
Broken bones or melanoma
would be a lot more simple.

The afternoon is hard to treat
and has no diagnosis.
The architects have done their bit though.

The ward is new and wide with light.

Geoff Page

To Drag the Saints back from Heaven

In the first week the saints will be available
only a little at a time. They will be busy
learning the names of things. Two or three
may attend memorials in their honour, but
you need to know you cannot count on this.

In the second week the saints will find heaven
heavy with rain as if they sat day after day
at the cyclone's fringe. They will not yet
know that this is grace and may try to return.
Do not drag them back with your prayers.

In the third week they will begin to forget
that heaven and earth were separated once.
They will spend all night and half the day
enthralled with the songs of frogs. If you make
your prayers amphibious, they may hear you.

But if, at the end of the third week, you drag
them back, you will see in their eyes they are
not yours. To keep them, you will need to feed
them cheese and bread, toast and jam, lentils
with brown rice, carrots and apples, a daily

bread in season. You will need to show them
things whose names heaven has not learnt:
the coastal banksia's bent answer to a place,
its shape against the sky. With spikes of
blossom you will pin them to your prayers.

Anne Elvey

True Listening in the Palace of Treasures

*Ling Lun, legendary founder of music theory in China, created pitch pipes
and discovered the ratios of the 12-tone scale (c. 27th Century BCE)*

Miserable— the cloud emperor who sits under
the tree of no music
                      seen in that seventh month
ruled by the breeze of the heart.

No appetite. No sleep.
                Slow breaths. His mind
assigning a passerby with the name of a bird—

Dark Bird Swallow, master of the equinox,
why do you perch on the sagging half-life?

As a remedy— Ling Lun, busy with bamboo,
cutting between knots, scraped and carving,
blew into hollows.

Birds gathered
               even the phoenix
ears uncoiling from their dark labyrinths.

Ling Lun's flute, watery cadence, his first note
aligned with the firmaments,
                 that same tenor of the bird.

Six notes for summer.
              Six notes for winter.

At this, how an emperor, all beings will travel
beyond the ordinary world—
                              with music,
the night arising from its prison to hold light
in trembling hands.

Michelle Leber

Twenty Questions

after Donald Justice

Is it constant in your land?
Does it rain constantly?
Are you a real character?
Have you ever got your hands dirty?
Is your passport current?
Are we closely related?
Do you honestly believe what you're saying?
Would you like to see the menu?
When did you last examine a scruple?
Have you ever forgotten your lines in public?

When were you last in the Holy Land?
Where is it precisely?
Are you a forerunner?
Have you ever been truly sorry?
Are you Cancer?
Do you worry about the future of the novel?
Have you found those binoculars?
Who watered the pitch in 1958?
Have you ever rhapsodised?
Would you mind completing a short survey?

Peter Rose

Under the Radar

Flaring and fading like the blips
That flash an instant on a radar screen,
The bellbirds' brilliant little flecks of sound
Illumine and eclipse
The points where silence has been slung between
The branches of the trees. Such flimsy tips
To bear the weight it gathers on the ground.

As when you wade through water, slowed
And heavy, hardly able to progress,
Your senses, working through this thick dimension
Of stillness, share its mode.
Each leaf glint, shadow, bird note, each impress
Of foot on twig that snaps beneath its load,
More slowly but more clearly holds attention.

Once all the world was this. Alone,
And dozing through the spell of midday heat,
You register that chittering outside,
A neighbour's telephone,
The drone of traffic on a further street,
The ticking house – each floated overtone
Dragged by the soundless groundswell that they ride.

And so it was when you were led
To where her barely conscious form lay waiting
And silence held the burden of the room.
And leaning by the bed,
You swayed in that abeyance, concentrating
To hear far off her scarcely warranted
And weightless breathing falter, and resume.

Stephen Edgar

Up at a Villa

So, it felt alright at first, but now you rabbit on
expressing indisputable views on everything, in vivid
agreement with yourself, reinforcing the big Yes,
it having been determined that all popes and poets
can be no more than cocksuckers, arseholes, or merely both.
You smile with anger, red behind rimless glasses,
and right. Well, you could hardly be wrong, eh?
Even the pleasant CD cannot stem your fucking flow;
I wouldn't dare to try, I tell you that.
Why is all this display of petty power so important
now to you: pretty well always has been. And why
does the furious cortex hunger after correctness,
in just about everything? Buggered if I know,
but it must have been much like this
ever since you swaggered out of your wicker cradle
and set about ruling the world; you had the measure
of left and right, art, money, sexual deviation
and all the main current of thought –
yes, I'll have another splash of the red, why not.

Your garden flourishes outside in fruitful technicolour,
skilfully maintained, of course, by those expert hands
while you see through the cloudy glass of each political party
as well as the seamiest anti-semites and mining thugs,
because you smell the due stink in everything,
the dirt that rots every pocket. Yes, you are bloody well like
those puritans you affect to hate so much, thin churchy rats.
Every phony, you force us to understand, has been fattened up
on taxpayers' money. No scholar is not a fake,
bar those few honest sods you happen to endorse
or at least agree with, today: those commonly known
as your disciples, docile ephebes and victims,

who wouldn't answer back in a month of Sundays.
We admire your dense green gardening, drink on,
nary a soul half-daring to answer back or argue – after all
who wants his or her noggin blasted off with a phrase
like fart-warmed thunder? Certainly not yours truly.
We'll go on laughing then into the deep lull of evening.
After all, tomorrow we're driving back to the city.

Chris Wallace-Crabbe

Valleys

(After Rimbaud)

The   hued emerald thickets of
desire to   lace fling themselves
have a cold like   at the vigilante
this one? in the air   doves i'the
ask the developed world   shade
about life & ambitions suffer   s
punishment for being a lovely per
son a weak friend this is not at   all
all a mass high-five even   people
fatigue mum said rest   dream of a
in bed or on a   sense of speed
bright me   a grouped psycho
ado   logical inheritance to
w   cut thru hazards & break up
            the walls of sound of atmospheric
u   bands on both sides of the rr
rude   room guards rotate like
waves of   news & elevate to
magic carpet   the top deck as I
produced real suns i   lluminate &
fire halfway up the walls   shift g
the attack of surround sound   ears
floodlights on the steering wheel
Amelie & I bounced behind   a
unclothed & breasted by   body
the waves at sea we   drew back
were done in   a view of dawn a
hull of a   black hearth & lamp
night   one reels as time wells

Toby Fitch

Warning

You slip the latch
and come to me across the ice.
A mouth is a circle lit
up, tapped out, departed.
Electrical haloes, we are
clairvoyant as soft gods,
sliding in boots, red stars on our soles.
We beckon dampness
into our woollens, swoop
an inner corona to the sheet-iron.

The memorial clock has no carillon.
There's a thread of you
on my collar when the nightwatchman
appears on the edge of the ice
to shout: *off, off,*
it won't hold you.

Ainslee Meredith

Watching How A Rain Front Stops

1

as it starts to do background
having been vertical drop down shutter-noise
leaf-quivering up to your neck in it soaking green
rainy earth-smoke and scarves upon boughs melting into air
melding into background of lost ridges beyond the paddocks
the air-wall of something not seen because you can't see it
last month's mirroring creek buried under mist with its blind flow
    between ponds,
re-growth bush on the far side and old, fenced land this side –
an overarching, moist clearness starting to saturate with blue-grey

2

within pale immensity which has permeated
the way the last ten minutes' change has occurred –
even the way each molecule of time was like a
snappy, wet branch swept across shoulder, through hair,
as I stepped back onto the verandah –
transformation happening as if marble turns to flesh
new breath on wet skin
while the threatening cloud-weight, bulging
across the range, starts to give way

3

to glinting bicycle spokes of once again look-alike daybreak light
through flecks of leaves, a
sudden spaciousness in the seeming quietness
(brooding quietness) (unstifled breathing calm)
the house   two fruiting quince trees   the shining spaniel

the loam's glint, drenched brilliant grass
and hardly to be noticed, the insects' rasp and saw
re-charging across edges and slopes
in the corners, low down, yet everywhere in

4

inertia and stillness, stilledness, everything happening
it blues the blueness growing,
so cleanly back of the mind we see things we don't see,
yet they're seen – a huge, untraceable lightness
remembered as an opening upwards   away over there
burnt paper climbing in a chimney's updraught
granulated sky with the suddenly sun-drenched grey heron
    picked out in the dam
– poster-paint grey wings, his neck "morning-after-a-snowstorm-
    in-Kosciuszko" whiteness –
flapping up in three, four, five alarmed strokes

Martin Harrison

Western landscapes with retreating horizons

The flurry of fingers on keyboards
spell silence, poets write
too late what time is and professors
dribble down murderous bibs:

There's no time to wonder
where time's gone

But the crowd shouts,
Wait a minute!
    turns sixty perfect circles

*

Shop bell rings, a knock on the door
Please shut down your power supply
we now own the sun. We bend over backwards
to comply, then bend over some more.

Cash registers ring *Hey, listen to this!*
police on radios, many countries mentioned
in one breath; one long breath drawn in
but never let out. We want to scream
what we know and release all the mice
from their treadmills. Ordinary indexes
swing through the trees and we hear the creaking
forest floor. Speeches die down to a low hum,
steal flight from everything feathered
and we pick wax stains from our wings.

*

The distant waves
  do what they do
and we set alight
  photographed catastrophes

When we rebuild, we won't govern
nor allow others the honour.
We'll live regretfully, we'll hoo ha

and dance a pirouette. No one
will notice. We'll explode in capital
letters all over the footpath,
croon old tunes to young audiences,
then forget how to bow. Once the jeering

dies down, we'll smile and show
each other scars. The crowd will cry
for more, then search us for knives.

                    *

Trumpets announce a recurring dream
of snow-capped mountains towering
over a wilderness of ideas.

You're from the past! a voice
down there cries, but we can't tell
if it's for us or the mountains.

This is the kind of confusion
sky must endure all the time.
The weight of the impossible
draped around a bird's neck
its clouded face dissolving

Once all the leaves are gathered
the mist will clear. We'll know
our real names and the sun
will be the busiest it's been

is the myth of circumstantial evidence
given the gift of happenstance:

There are no further hiding places
now the earth beneath our feet
is ploughed, and the planet's
axis is the balance beam on which
we take our final bow.

Paul Mitchell

Whale Heart

An album of photocopies of photographs of
the ancestors. A woman whose face is always

scratched out. The interior of the once-beautiful
church. Young men on the deck of a whaling boat

cutting the tail and fins from a captive humpback;
a crude blade attached to a long wooden pole. The

whale still alive while this happens, though weak
enough to be lashed to the side of the boat. The

boys pose shirtless, triumphant around the immense
carcass, their lean arms around each other's shoulders.

We try to make out which organ lies at their feet.
How big is the heart of a whale? But not one of us knows.

Josephine Rowe

What Frances Farmer Ate

Nobody knows I'm here. Abscond of old,
this gold hair celluloid loves to capture
silenced by a dowdy scarf.

Into the brown-skinned night-market crowd
I go, buy an egg from someone crying *balut!*
Crack it open. Inside, the embryo
duckling feathered in soupy broth,
unseeing eye a full stop.
Have you ever had a broken heart?
I drink its liquid with a pinch of salt
and remembered when I wrote 'God Dies' one broken night.
Those ballerinas in Russia can't dance me out of this
idea: *I blame nobody for my fall.*
I open my mouth,
swallow the contents whole.

Ivy Alvarez

When God Dies

So let's get this straight:

       We don't do state funerals –

but what we do do,
       is tabloid extravaganzas starring Valmae Beck?
– *& hasn't prison aged the old duck terribly!*

       Isn't it enough that we have already
diminished ourselves?
We are fallen with no path to redemption,
why bother with the hairshirt?

       The film I will never sees stars George Eastman
hair grown long & saltwater thick
after a summer lazy in the Balearics.

Lensed by Polanski, an Alan Smithee stand in
       for Joe D'Amato

& Anna Karina fresh from Godard
goes under the axe blade in this
sub B-Grade faux-Bergman B&W shocker.

& I stick to my guns
because the newspapers in this town
       only report reliably
on gossip, slander & opinion.

Liam Ferney

When You Showed Me the Stars

The moon hung from the sky like a dead thing
You tried to show me the stars again
But this time I was not listening

Your face already turned towards somewhere else
The horizon surrendering one bare tree
Scared white in the moonlight

So we sat in the silent blue
"It's okay, I half-expected this"
And I wasn't lying but it still came as a shock

The next morning when you were gone
The tired wire-screen door closed so violently behind me
Red dirt blew in and suddenly it hurt.

Gemma White

Who Took the Bee's Greed For a Sign

Who took the bee's greed for a sign,
who through a point drew a straight line,
who opened the eyes to malicious things,
who taught rapier to the strings?

Who flattens childhood's eager grass,
who hopes the dream will quickly pass,
who recollects the border train,
who warns of death and life again?

Eugene Dubnov
Translated from the Russian by **Peter Porter** *with the author*

Window onto the Bay (*after Kafka*)

Whoever could sit in solitude by a window looking out over the sullen bay and yet people it with sea weary sailors, gulls screeching overhead, terns darting swiftly, deftly; solemnly protecting their cliff-side nests and where swallows dot a dreary skyline like coursing black stars in the daytime; the solitary watcher will never be lonely nor will she ever fail to craft a poem that will hook the reader of fine words with a relentless tackle to be reeled in breathless on a pebbly shore nor will she fail to pierce the mirror of that reader's illusions with sharp intonations, striated synaesthesia perhaps on a drunken boat, perhaps the corpse of a cross bowed albatross and the dart of her desire (whatever it is; fame, strength, to walk straight on a crooked dune path) will arch over that sheltered rocky cliff: it may drop sharp into the dark green-kelped depth or it may land softly on a ledge swept by the kestrel so vigilant over its crag nest. I am thinking of Kafka in Prague: of his window onto the street.

Christopher Konrad

Women in Classical Chinese Love Poems

are always waiting
under moonlight
with cloud-damp hair.
Moth eyebrows signify
their great beauty.
Nothing occupies them more
than crickets and longing –
time passed in cicada-hours,
cups of undrunk tea.
Come evening, their beds grow
full of one-way love.
With no shoulder to cry upon,
instead the candles weep
until cold hours of dawn.
Dew is their abundance.
Sitting, standing, reclining:
these are the classic positions.
From girlhood they have known
grief must be sung, all hope
arrives on a west wind.
Persimmon-lipped, they live
by windows: flowering, fruiting,
composing slowly to stone.

Debbie Lim

Publication Details

Robert Adamson's 'Francis Webb at Ball's Head' appeared in the *Australian Poetry Journal*, vol. 2 (2), 2012.

Adam Aitken's 'Old Europe (2)' appeared in *Overland*, vol. 208, Spring 2012.

Ali Alizadeh's 'Spiritual' appeared in the *Age*, 8 September 2012.

Ivy Alvarez's 'What Frances Farmer Ate' appeared in *Three Chords and the Truth: Etchings* 11, Ilura Press, 2012.

Chris Andrews' 'Mateship' appeared in *Contrappasso Magazine*, vol. 2, 2013.

Cassandra Atherton's 'P.R.B' appeared in *Australian Book Review*, May 2013.

Peter Bakowski's 'City workers during morning rush hour, Collins Street, Melbourne, 2013' appeared (in an earlier version) on the *Eureka Street* website, September 2012.

Judith Beveridge's 'A Dire Season' appeared in *The Warwick Review*, vol. 6 (2), 2012.

Kim Cheng Boey's 'Chinatowns', from which this excerpt was taken, appeared in his collection *Clear Brightness* (Puncher & Wattman, 2012; Epigram Books [Singapore], 2012).

Ken Bolton's '"Hindley Street": How to Be Perfect There' appeared in *Cordite Poetry Review*, Issue 43.0: Masque, 2013.

Michael Brennan's 'Autoethnographic' appeared in his collection *Autoethnographic* (Giramondo, 2012).

Lachlan Brown's 'Outstretched Arms' appeared in his collection *Limited Cities* (Giramondo, 2012).

Pam Brown's 'Closed on Mondays' appeared in *Otoliths*, vol. 29, 2013. Acknowledgement: thanks to Iain Sinclair and *Art Monthly* magazine.

Melinda Bufton's 'Did you mean *iteration?*' appeared in the *Age*, 12 January 2013.

Michelle Cahill's 'Renovations' appeared in the *Age*, 2 February 2013.

Justin Clemens' 'Blind Spot' appeared in *Southerly*, vol. 72 (2), 2012.

Jennifer Compton's 'Sorrowful' appeared in *Australian Book Review*, March 2013.

Nathan Curnow's 'Prophecy' appeared in *Australian Book Review*, March 2013.

Sarah Day's 'Dawn' appeared in the *Age*, 27 April 2013, and in her collection *Tempo* (Puncher & Wattman, 2013).

Brett Dionysius's 'Black Throated Finch' appeared in *The Disappearing*, an app published by The Red Room Company, 2012.

Dan Disney's 'A Quick Drink at the Bar' appeared in the *Australian Poetry Journal*, vol. 2 (2), 2012. The poem responds to an interview with Robert Creeley, which appeared in *Paris Review*, no. 44, Fall 1968.

Laurie Duggan's 'An Ordinary Evening in Newtown' appeared in *Australian Book Review*, April 2013.

Daniel East's 'The God of Bone and Antler' appeared in *Contrappasso Magazine*, vol. 2, 2013.

Will Eaves' 'Dandelion' appeared in the *Age*, 2 August 2013.

Ali Cobby Eckermann's 'Ochre' appeared in her collection *Ruby Moonlight* (Magabala Books, 2012).

Anne Elvey's 'To Drag the Saints back from Heaven' appeared in *Meanjin*, vol. 72 (2), 2013.

Russell Erwin's 'As Flames Were My Only Witness' appeared in *Meanjin*, vol. 72 (1), 2013.

Diane Fahey's 'On Dreams' appeared in the *Age*, 16 March 2013.

Michael Farrell's 'Not in Vain' appeared in the *Age*, 13 April 2013.

Susan Fealy's 'Bringing You Home' appeared in *Rabbit*, vol. 6, 2012.

Anna Fern's 'Strange, unremarkably so' appeared in the Queensland Poetry Festival's *Spoken in One Strange Word: Anthology 2013*.

Liam Ferney's 'When God Dies' appeared in *Rabbit*, vol. 5, 2012.

Lionel G. Fogarty's 'Induct True Legendary Thrills Bravery' appeared in *Island*, vol. 132, Autumn 2013.

Claire Gaskin's 'pollen wind' appeared in *Southerly*, vol. 72 (2), 2012.

Robert Gray's 'The Dark Sisters' appeared in *Contrappasso Magazine*, vol. 2, 2013.

Kevin Hart's 'Little Book of Mourning' appeared in *Westerly*, vol. 58 (1), 2013.

John Hawke's 'The Conscience of Avimael Guzman' appeared in *Cordite Poetry Review*, Issue 41.1: Ratbaggery, 2013.

Paul Hetherington's 'Five Abstractions of Blue' appeared in his collection *Six Different Windows* (UWA Publishing, 2013).

Fiona Hile's 'The inevitable beauty of the viewer when faced with the partitionist tactics of the situationist lover' appeared in the *Age*, 11 May 2013.

Sarah Holland-Batt's 'Last Goodbyes in Havana' appeared in the *Australian Poetry Journal*, vol. 2 (2), 2012.

L. K. Holt's *Stages of Balthazar (with a Chorus of Elders)* was published by Vagabond Press (Rare Object Series) in 2013.

Darby Hudson's 'Lumière Train' appeared in Troublemag.com in September 2012.

Andy Jackson's 'Edith' appeared in the *Australian Poetry Journal*, vol. 2 (2), 2012.

Clive James' 'Leçons de Ténèbres', first published in the *New Yorker*, 3 June 2013 (Copyright © Clive James, 2013), is reproduced by permission of United Agents (www.unitedagents.co.uk) on behalf of Clive James.

Ella Jeffery's 'The Brooklyn International Motel' appeared in *Voiceworks*, vol. 93, Winter 2013.

Jill Jones' 'The Slide' appeared in *Westerly*, vol. 57 (2), 2012.

Paul Kane's 'Co. Kerry' appeared in *Australian Book Review*, September 2012.

Carmen Leigh Keates' '*Nostalghia*' appeared in the *Australian Poetry Journal*, vol. 2 (2), 2012.

Kit Kelen's 'the dead are with us' and 'you read it here' appeared in *Island*, vol. 132, Autumn 2013.

John Kinsella's 'Bushfire Approaching' appeared in *Australian Book Review*, March 2013.

Andy Kissane's 'My Husband's Grave' appeared in *Cordite Poetry Review*, Issue 40.1: Indonesia, 2012.

Shari Kocher's 'my singing empty hands' appeared in *Cordite Poetry Review*, Issue 40.0: Interlocutor, 2012.

Christopher Konrad's 'Window onto the Bay (after Kafka)' appeared in *Westerly*, vol. 57 (2), 2012.

Jo Langdon's 'Ellipsis' appeared in *Cordite Poetry Review*, Issue 40.0: Interlocutor, 2012.

Anthony Lawrence's 'Poetry of the Taliban' appeared in the *Australian Poetry Journal*, vol. 2 (2), 2012.

Michelle Leber's 'True Listening in the Palace of Treasures' appeared in *Three Chords and the Truth: Etchings* 11, Ilura Press, 2012.

Bella Li's 'Drowning Dream' appeared in the collection *Contemporary Asian Australian Poets* (Puncher & Wattman, 2013). Its first sentence is a variation on the line 'This August I began to dream of drowning', from Anne Sexton's poem 'Imitations of Drowning'.

Rosanna Licari's 'Revisiting Yugoslavia: *Rijeka, Croatia*' appeared in the *Australian Poetry Journal*, vol. 2 (2), 2012.

Kate Lilley's 'Season's Greetings' appeared in *Southerly*, vol. 72 (2), 2012.

Debbie Lim's 'Women in Classical Chinese Love Poems' also appears in *Australian Love Poems 2013*, edited by Mark Tredinnick (Inkerman & Blunt, 2013).

Cameron Lowe's 'Rise and Shine' appeared in *Cordite Poetry Review*, Issue 41.1: Ratbaggery, 2013.

Paul Magee's 'Rupert in Japan' appeared in *Burley Journal*, no. 4, 2013.

Mark Mahemoff's 'Hotel' appeared in the *Age*, 15 September 2012.

Jennifer Maiden's 'Diary Poem: Uses of Frank O'Hara' appeared in *Australian Book Review*, June 2013.

David Malouf's 'At Lerici' appeared in his collection *Sky News* (Vagabond Press Rare Object Series, 2013).

Ainslee Meredith's 'Warning' appeared in her collection *Pinetorch* (Express Media/Australian Poetry, 2013).

Kate Middleton's 'Ephemeral Waters' appeared in her collection *Ephemeral Waters* (Giramondo, 2013).

Peter Minter's 'The Roadside Bramble' appeared in *Southerly*, vol. 72 (1), 2012.

Paul Mitchell's 'Western Landscapes with Retreating Horizons' appeared in *Westerly*, vol. 58 (1), 2013.

Les Murray's 'A Denizen' appeared in *Australian Book Review*, March 2013.

David Musgrave's 'Coastline' appeared in the *Newcastle Poetry Prize Anthology 2012*.

Nguyen Tien Hoang's 'Summer' appeared in the *Age*, 15 June 2013.

Jal Nicholl's 'As in the future when' appeared in the *Age*, 2 March 2013.

Ella O'Keefe's 'Basic Hut Methodology' appeared in *Cordite Poetry Review*, Issue 41.1: Ratbaggery, 2013.

Louise Oxley's 'The Bat Corridor' appeared on the *Cordite Poetry Review* website, 15 July 2013.

Geoff Page's 'The Ward Is New' appeared in *Meanjin*, vol. 72 (1), 2013.

π.O.'s 'Street Encounter' appeared in *Southerly*, vol. 72 (1), 2012.

Peter Porter's 'Who Took the Bee's Greed for a Sign' (translated from the Russian with the author, Eugene Dubnov) appeared in *Westerly*, vol. 58 (1), 2013.

Claire Potter's 'Plant Poem' appeared in the *Age*, 3 November 2012.

Judith Rodriguez's 'The Life Inside' appeared in *Island*, vol. 131, Summer 2012.

Aden Rolfe's 'Regression to the Mean' appeared in the *Age*, 19 January 2013.

Josephine Rowe's 'Whale Heart' is an excerpt from her 'Bar Haven Suite', which appeared in *Offset*, vol. 12, October 2012.

Robyn Rowland's 'Shaping the Dark: Three Readings of Tony Lloyd's Oil on Linen Painting "On a Dark Night You Can See Forever"', from which the excerpt featured in this volume was taken, appeared in *Westerly*, vol. 57 (2), 2012.

Brendan Ryan's 'Succession', from which the excerpt featured in this volume was taken, appeared in *Westerly*, vol. 58 (1), 2013.

Gig Ryan's 'Rally' appeared in *Text*, Special Issue Website Series, no. 17, April 2013.

Tracy Ryan's 'Dual Citizen' appeared in her collection *Unearthed* (Fremantle Press, 2013).

Andrew Sant's 'Mediterranean Time' appeared in the *Weekend Australian Review*, 25 May 2013.

Brenda Saunders' 'Inside Edward Hopper' appeared in the *Australian Poetry Journal*, vol. 2 (2), 2012, and in her collection *the sound of red* (Ginninderra Press, 2013).

Oscar Schwartz's 'Nyirbator' appeared in the *Age*, 9 February 2013.

Thomas Shapcott's 'The Owl Painting' appeared in the *Age*, 30 March 2013.

Laura Jan Shore's 'Revealed' appeared in *Westerly*, vol. 58 (1), 2013.

James Stuart's 'Postcard for Marilla' appeared in his collection *Imitation Era* (Vagabond Press Rare Object Series, 2012), and will also appear in his forthcoming book *Anonymous Folk Songs* (Vagabond Press).

Maria Takolander's 'Chimney' appeared in *Meanjin*, vol. 72 (2), 2013.

John Tranter's 'Crowded Hour' appeared in the *Times Literary Supplement*, 12 July 2013; 'The Consonants' appeared in *Australian Book Review*, May 2013.

Ann Vickery's 'Another Chardin in Need of Cleaning' appeared in *Cordite Poetry Review*, Issue 42.0: No Theme II, 2013.

Corey Wakeling's 'The Ear Especially' appeared in *Overland*, vol. 209, Summer 2012, and in his collection *Goad Omen* (Giramondo, 2013).

Chris Wallace-Crabbe's 'Up at a Villa' appeared in his collection *New and Selected Poems* (Carcanet Press, 2013).

Alan Wearne's 'The Vanity of Australian Wishes', from which this excerpt is taken, appeared in his collection *Prepare the Cabin for Landing* (Giramondo, 2012).

Gemma White's 'When You Showed Me the Stars' appeared in the *Age*, 16 February 2013.

Jessica L. Wilkinson's 'Jivin' with Bonny Cassidy etc.' appeared in *Cordite Poetry Review*, Issue 41.1: Ratbaggery, 2013.

R. D. Wood's 'In the Desert' appeared in *Southerly*, vol. 72 (1), 2012.

Ouyang Yu's translation of Bai Helin's 'Meeting with the Same River' appeared in the *Age*, 10 November 2012; his translation of Hu Xian's 'The Orchard' appeared in the *Age*, 20 April 2013.

Notes on Contributors

The Editor

Lisa Gorton lives in Melbourne. She studied at the universities of Melbourne and Oxford and wrote a doctorate on John Donne's poetry and prose. She was awarded the John Donne Society Award for Distinguished Publication in Donne Studies. Lisa's first poetry collection, *Press Release* (Giramondo, 2007), won the Victorian Premier's Prize for Poetry, the C.J. Dennis Award. Lisa has also been awarded the Vincent Buckley Poetry Prize. Her poetry collection *Hotel Hyperion*, also from Giramondo, came out in 2013 and was shortlisted for the Queensland Literary Awards.

Poets

Robert Adamson has published over twenty books of poetry, including the triple prize-winning 1990 collection *The Clean Dark*. His autobiography, *Inside Out*, was published in 2004. In 2011 he was awarded the Patrick White Award and the Blake Prize for Poetry. His latest book of poetry, *The Kingfisher's Soul*, was published by Bloodaxe Books in 2009.

Adam Aitken has been a printer's assistant, a poetry magazine editor and a PhD student. He is the author of four books of poetry and four chapbooks, most recently *Eighth Habitation* (Giramondo, 2009) and *November Already* (Vagabond Press, 2013). He teaches cultural studies and academic literacy at UTS.

Ali Alizadeh's last collection of poetry, *Ashes in the Air* (UQP, 2011) was shortlisted for the Prime Minister's Literary Award, Poetry. His new book is a work of fiction, *Transactions* (UQP, 2013). He is a lecturer in literature and creative writing at Monash University.

Ivy Alvarez is the author of *Disturbance* (Seren, 2013) and *Mortal* (2006). A recipient of writing residencies from MacDowell Colony,

Hawthornden Castle and Fundación Valparaiso, her work appears in journals and anthologies in many countries and online, with individual poems translated into Russian, Spanish, Japanese and Korean. www.ivyalvarez.com.

Chris Andrews teaches at the University of Western Sydney. He has published two books of poems – *Cut Lunch* (Indigo, 2002) and *Lime Green Chair* (Waywiser, 2012) – and has translated books of Latin American fiction, including Roberto Bolaño's *By Night in Chile* (New Directions, 2003) and César Aira's *Shantytown* (New Directions, 2013).

Louis Armand is a Sydney-born writer who lives in Prague. He is the editor of *Contemporary Poetics* (Northwestern, 2007). His most recent collections of poetry are *Letters from Ausland* (Vagabond Press, 2011) and *Synopticon* (with John Kinsella, LPB, 2012). He is an editor of the *VLAK* magazine.

Cassandra Atherton has published a book of poetry, *After Lolita* (Ahadada Press, 2010), a novel, *The Man Jar* (Printed Matter Press, 2010) and a book of literary criticism. Her book of interviews with American public intellectuals, *In So Many Words*, is forthcoming from Australian Scholarly Publishing. See her website for more information: www.cassandra-atherton.com.

Bai Helin, whose real name is Tang Ruibing, was born in Pengxi, Sichuan, China, in 1973. He began publishing poetry in 1993 and has been widely published in China, won many prizes and published a number of poetry books, including *chexing tuzhong* (*Travelling by Train on the Way*).

Peter Bakowski has been writing poetry for over thirty years. He keeps in mind the following three quotes: 'Use ordinary words to say extraordinary things' – Arthur Schopenhauer; 'Writing is painting' – Charles Bukowski; and 'Make your next poem different from your last' – attributed to Robert Frost. In 2014 Hunter Publishers will publish *Personal Weather*, his fifth poetry title.

Judith Beveridge is the author of *The Domesticity of Giraffes, Accidental Grace, Wolf Notes* and *Storm and Honey*, all of which have won major prizes. Her new collection will be published by Giramondo in 2014. She is the poetry editor for *Meanjin* and teaches poetry writing at postgraduate level at the University of Sydney.

Kim Cheng Boey has published five collections of poetry and a travel memoir. He emigrated from Singapore in 1997, and currently teaches creative writing at the University of Newcastle.

A gay, light-hearted bastard, **Ken Bolton** cuts a moodily romantic figure within the dun Australian literary landscape, his name inevitably conjuring perhaps that best known image of him, bow-tie askew, grinning cheerfully, at the wheel of his 1955 Jaguar D-type, *El Cid*.

Michael Brennan lives in Tokyo, where he is an associate professor in the Faculty of Policy Studies, Chuo University, and runs Vagabond Press (www.vagabondpress.net). His most recent collection is *Autoethnographic* (Giramondo, 2012), versions of which are also being published in Vietnamese and Japanese.

David Brooks' latest collection is the highly acclaimed *The Balcony* (UQP, 2008). A new collection, *Open House*, will be published by UQP in early 2015. His most recent publication is the novel *The Conversation* (UQP, 2012). He is an honorary associate professor at the University of Sydney, and co-editor of *Southerly*.

Lachlan Brown currently lectures in English literature and creative writing at Charles Sturt University, Wagga. He grew up in south-west Sydney and his poems have appeared in journals such as *Heat*, *Mascara*, *Westside* and *Relief*. Lachlan's first volume of poetry, *Limited Cities*, was published by Giramondo in 2012.

Pam Brown has published many books and chapbooks, most recently *More than a feuilleton* (Little Esther, 2012) and *Home by Dark* (Shearsman, 2013). She divides her time between Zlín, Moravia, and Alexandria, Sydney.

Melinda Bufton is a Melbourne poet and reviewer. Her work has appeared in a number of publications, including *Cordite*, *Rabbit*, the *Age* and (translated) the Chinese poetry journal *Du Shi*. Her debut collection is forthcoming from Inken Publisch (www.inkenpublisch. com).

Joanne Burns is a Sydney poet. Her most recent poetry collection is *amphora* (Giramondo, 2011). 'snowy' is included in a new poetry manuscript, *brush*, which she is currently assembling.

Michelle Cahill is a Sydney poet. Her collection *Vishvarūpa* (Five Islands Press, 2012) was shortlisted in the Victorian Premier's Literary Awards. She received the Val Vallis Award and is the CAL/UOW Fellow at Kingston University, London. Her fiction and essays appear in *Southerly, Westerly, Antipodes* and *Wasafiri*.

Bonny Cassidy is a Melbourne poet, essayist and reviewer. Her debut collection, *Certain Fathoms* (Puncher & Wattmann, 2012), was shortlisted for the WA Premier's Book Awards, and she has a second book forthcoming from Giramondo in early 2014.

Justin Clemens' most recent books are *Psychoanalysis is an Antiphilosophy* (Edinburgh University Press, 2013) and a new, expanded version of his mock-epic poem *The Mundiad* (Hunter Publishing, 2013). He teaches at the University of Melbourne.

Jennifer Compton lives in Melbourne and is a poet and playwright who also writes prose. Her book of poetry *Barefoot* (Picaro Press, 2010) was shortlisted for the John Bray Award, and *This City* (Otago University Press, 2011) won the Kathleen Grattan Award. *Ungainly* came out in 2012 with Mulla Mulla Press.

Nathan Curnow is an award-winning poet and past editor of *Going Down Swinging*. He was recently described by Martin Duwell as 'a sort of poetic equivalent of Louis Theroux'. His books include *No Other Life But This* (Five Islands Press), *The Ghost Poetry Project* (Puncher & Wattmann) and *RADAR* (Walleah Press).

Sarah Day's most recent book is *Tempo* (Puncher & Wattmann, 2013). Awards for her work include the Judith Wright Calanthe Queensland Premier's Award, the Judith Wright ACT, the University of Melbourne Wesley Michelle Wright Prize and the Anne Elder Award. She lives in Hobart, where she teaches Year 12 creative writing.

Brett Dionysius was founding director of the Queensland Poetry Festival. His poetry has been widely published in literary journals, anthologies, newspapers and online. His eighth poetry collection, *Weranga*, was released in August 2013. He lives in Ipswich, Queensland, where he runs, watches birds, teaches English and writes sonnets.

Dan Disney has published poems, reviews, and essays on contemporary poetry and creativity in journals in Australia, Europe and

Britain. His collection of poems, *and then when the,* was published by John Leonard Press in 2011. He teaches at Sogang University in Seoul, Korea, in the English literature program.

Eugene Dubnov was born in Tallinn, and educated at Moscow and London universities. Two collections of his poems in Russian came out in London; his verse and prose in English translation and written in English have appeared in many periodicals and anthologies. His recent poetry collection in English, *The Thousand-Year Minutes,* was published by Shoestring Press in 2013.

Laurie Duggan was born in Melbourne and has lived in Sydney, Canberra and Brisbane. In 2006 he moved to England, where he lives in a market town in East Kent. His most recent volumes are *The Pursuit of Happiness* (Shearsman, 2012) and *The Collected Blue Hills* (Puncher & Wattman, 2012).

Daniel East is an Australian writer currently working in Sydney. His work has appeared in *Cordite, Mascara, Going Down Swinging, cut-throat, Contrappasso, Voiceworks, Red River Review* and *Verity La.* He co-wrote *Sexy Tales of Paleontology,* which won the 2010 Sydney Fringe Comedy Award. Perhaps you'd like to follow his informal Tumblr, damnnearhysteria?

Will Eaves is the author of three novels, most recently *This Is Paradise* (2012), and a collection of poetry, *Sound Houses* (2011). He was arts editor of the *Times Literary Supplement* for many years and now teaches at the University of Warwick.

Ali Cobby Eckermann is a poet and memoirist. Her collections of verse include *little bit long time* (Australian Poetry Centre, 2010), *Kami* (Vagabond Press, 2010) and *Love dreaming & other poems* (Vagabond Press, 2012). Her two verse novels are *His Father's Eyes* (Oxford University Press, 2011) and *Ruby Moonlight* (Magabala Books, 2012).

Stephen Edgar's most recent collection is *Eldershaw* (Black Pepper). In 2012 *The Red Sea: New and Selected Poems* (Baskerville) was published in the US. A new collection, *Exhibits of the Sun,* is due out from Black Pepper in late 2013.

Chris Edwards is the Sydney-based author of *A Fluke* (Monogene and Jacket, 2006) and *People of Earth* (Vagabond Press, 2011). His poems are sometimes built around (mis)quotations from what he calls 'sources' – in this case, Timothy Ferris, *Coming of Age in the Milky Way*, and P. D. James, *A Dalgliesh Trilogy*.

Anne Elvey is author of three chapbooks, including *Bent toward the thing* (2012). She has a full-length collection forthcoming from Five Islands Press in 2014. Anne is managing editor of *Plumwood Mountain: An Australian Journal of Ecopoetry and Ecopoetics* and holds honorary appointments at Monash University and MCD University of Divinity.

Russell Erwin farms in the Southern Tablelands of New South Wales, near where wind towers are crowding the sky, 'farming' it.

Diane Fahey's *The Wing Collection* (Puncher & Wattmann, 2011) was shortlisted for the 2012 Adelaide Festival of Arts' John Bray Poetry Award. Her most recent collection is *The Stone Garden* (Clouds of Magellan, 2013). Diane has won the Newcastle Poetry Prize, the Wesley Michel Wright Award and the ACT Judith Wright Poetry Prize. She took part in the Australian Poetry Tour of Ireland in May/June, 2013.

Michael Farrell was born in Bombala, New South Wales, and lives in Melbourne. His latest book is *Open Sesame* (Giramondo, 2012).

Susan Fealy is a poet and clinical psychologist. This year her poetry has appeared in *Australian Love Poems 2013, Australian Poetry Journal, Eureka Street, Mascara Literary Review* and *Rabbit*, and was awarded the 2013 NSW Society of Women Writers National Poetry Prize. She is working towards her first full-length collection.

Anna Fern lives and works as an editor in Melbourne. She crosses between spoken word and sound poetry, and loves plucking sounds from unlikely objects. Her new CD *Mouthful* is available at annafern@alphalink.com.au.

Liam Ferney lives in Brisbane and works in media management. His second full-length collection of poetry, *Boom*, was published by Grand Parade Poets in 2013. He was Poetry Editor of *Cordite Poetry Review* in 2004–05.

Toby Fitch is based in Sydney. His book *Rawshock* (Puncher & Wattmann) was co-winner of the 2012 Grace Leven Prize for Poetry. He is currently the poetry reviews editor for *Southerly* and a doctoral candidate at the University of Sydney. He is working on his next book of poems, a book of inversions.

Lionel G. Fogarty was born in 1958 at Barambah, now known as Cherbourg Aboriginal Reserve, in the South Burnett region of southern Queensland. His first collection of poetry, *Kargun*, was published in 1980. He has since published eight collections, as well as a children's book, *Booyooburra*, a traditional Wakka Wakka story.

Angela Gardner has written two books of poetry: *Views of the Hudson* (Shearsman Press, 2009), and the 2006 Arts Queensland Thomas Shapcott Poetry Prize winner *Parts of Speech* (University of Queensland Press, 2007). She is currently Australian Poetry's Café Poet in Residence at the Gallery of Modern Art, Brisbane.

Claire Gaskin's poetry collection *A Bud* was shortlisted in the *John Bray SA Festival Award for Literature* in 2008. She has been teaching creative writing and literature for twenty-five years. Her new collection, entitled *Paperweight*, is forthcoming with Hunter Publishers in its Australian Poetry Series 2013.

Jane Gibian is a poet and librarian whose publications include *tidemark* (Vagabond Press, 2013) and *Ardent* (Giramondo, 2007). Her work has been widely anthologised, most recently in *Thirty Australian Poets* (UQP, 2011) and *Australian Poetry Since 1788* (UNSW Press, 2011).

Robert Gray has recently published, with George Braziller in New York, a selection of his poems, *Daylight Saving*. His collected poems, *Cumulus*, was published in Australia in 2012.

Tim Grey is a writer, journalist and photographer from Melbourne. His poetry has appeared in publications such as *Southerly, Rabbit* and *Mascara*.

Poet and essayist **Martin Harrison**'s most recent book of poems is *Living Things: Five Poems* (Vagabond Press, 2013). His volume of selected poems is *Wild Bees: New and Selected Poems* (UWA Press, 2008). He has been widely translated into Chinese, and a French edition of his work is forthcoming.

Kevin Hart's most recent collection of poems is *Morning Knowledge* (Notre Dame University Press, 2011). He is currently completing a new book of poems, *Barefoot*. He teaches at the University of Virginia.

John Hawke is a Sydney poet, currently teaching in the English department at Monash University.

Paul Hetherington is the author of ten collections of poetry, including *Six Different Windows* (UWA Publishing, 2013). He was recently shortlisted for the 2013 Newcastle Poetry Prize and longlisted for the 2013 Montreal International Poetry Prize. He edited three volumes of Donald Friend's diaries and is head of the International Poetry Studies Institute.

Fiona Hile is the author of a chapbook, *The Family Idiot*, and a full-length collection, *Novelties*. In 2012 she won the *Island* Gwen Harwood Poetry Prize and was awarded second place in the *Overland* Judith Wright Poetry Prize. Her poems have been published in the *Age, Overland, Shearsman, Cordite* and elsewhere.

Matt Holden is a freelance journalist and editor who also writes poetry and short fiction. He lives in Melbourne.

Sarah Holland-Batt's first book, *Aria* (UQP, 2008), was the recipient of the Thomas Shapcott Prize, the Arts ACT Judith Wright Poetry Prize and the F. A. W. Anne Elder Award. In late 2013 she will take up a MacDowell Fellowship in New Hampshire.

L. K. Holt's first collection, *Man Wolf Man*, received the Kenneth Slessor Prize, and her second, *Patience, Mutiny*, received the Grace Leven Prize. *Stages of Balthazar* was published as a chapbook by Vagabond Press: part one includes within the chorus some loose adaptations of lines from Rilke's *Sonnets to Orpheus*.

Hu Xian, born in 1966 and now resident in Nanjing, China, has won many major poetry prizes, such as the Wen Yiduo Poetry Prize, and published a number of poetry books, such as *zhenyu* (*Shower*) and *shinian deng* (*A Decade of Lamps*).

Darby Hudson is a writer/illustrator from Melbourne and a regular contributor to Troublemag.com. He also had a poem in *The Best Australian Poems 2012*. www.darbyhudson.com.

Andy Jackson's *Among the Regulars* (papertiger, 2010) was shortlisted for the Kenneth Slessor Prize and Highly Commended in the Anne Elder Award. Recent poems have appeared in *Meanjin, The Best Australian Poems 2012* and *Medical Journal of Australia*. He is currently writing a series of portrait poems of people with Marfan Syndrome. amongtheregulars.wordpress.com.

Clive James is an Australian writer who lives in Cambridge, England. His poem 'Leçons de Ténèbres' was first published in the *New Yorker*. His latest book is a translation of the *Divine Comedy*.

Ella Jeffery's poetry and short fiction have appeared in *Cordite*, *Voiceworks*, *Stilts* and other journals. She was born on the far north coast of New South Wales and recently graduated from Queensland University of Technology's creative writing program.

A. Frances Johnson's poetry has appeared in *The Best Australian Poems 2009, 2010* and *2011*. She has published two books of poetry, *The Pallbearer's Garden* (Whitmore Press, 2008) and *The Wind-up Birdman of Moorabool Street* (Puncher & Wattmann, 2012), which received the 2012 Michel Wesley Wright Prize. She teaches at the University of Melbourne.

Jill Jones' recent books include *Ash is Here, So are Stars* (2012) and *Dark Bright Doors* (2010). An e-chapbook, *even if the signal fails*, is forthcoming from Black Rider Press, and a new full-length book, *The Beautiful Anxiety*, is due from Puncher & Wattmann in early 2014. She is a member of the J. M. Coetzee Centre for Creative Practice, University of Adelaide.

Paul Kane has published five collections of poems and, most recently, a CD: S*even Catastrophes in Four Movements* (Farpoint Recordings). He serves as poetry editor for *Antipodes*, artistic director for the Mildura Writers Festival, and general editor for The Braziller Series of Australian Poets. He teaches at Vassar.

Carmen Leigh Keates was shortlisted for the 2013 ACU Literature Prize, the 2012 Whitmore Press Manuscript Prize and the 2011 Alec Bolton Prize for an Unpublished Manuscript. Some of her poems appear in recent issues of the *Australian Poetry Journal*. Keates is completing her PhD at the University of Queensland.

Christopher (Kit) Kelen is a poet, scholar and visual artist who shuttles between his home at Markwell via Bulahdelah and a position as Professor of English at the University of Macau in South China. His next volume of poems, *Scavenger's Season*, will be published by Puncher & Wattman in 2014.

John Kinsella the author of numerous volumes of poetry including *Armour* (Picador, 2011) and *Jam Tree Gully* (W. W. Norton, 2012). He is a Fellow of Churchill College, Cambridge University, and a Professorial Research Fellow at the University of Western Australia. He is poetry editor for *Island* magazine.

Andy Kissane was the winner of the 2013 Fish International Poetry Prize and is the 2013 Coriole National Wine Poet, with six of his poems featuring on the back label of the vinyard's cabernet shiraz. His fourth collection of poetry, *Radiance*, will be published by Puncher & Wattmann in 2014. andykissane.com.

Shari Kocher's poetry is widely published in literary journals in Australia and elsewhere. Her first book, *The Non-Sequitur of Snow,* is forthcoming with Puncher & Wattmann. Her current creative project *Sonqoqui* comprises part of her doctoral research toward her PhD candidature at Melbourne University. Shari lives in the Yarra Valley. Her website is a work in progress: www.carapacedreaming.wordpress.

Christopher Konrad completed his PhD in creative writing at Edith Cowan University in 2012. His work has been published in *Sandfire* (Sunline Press, 2011) and in many journals and online, and has won the Tom Collins Prize (2009) and the Todhunter Literary Award (2012). He currently works with a migrant settlement service in Perth.

Jo Langdon is the author of a poetry chapbook, *Snowline* (Whitmore Press, 2012). She lives in Geelong and is currently completing a PhD at Deakin University.

Anthony Lawrence's most recent collection of poems is *Signal Flare* (Puncher & Wattmann, 2013). He teaches Creative Writing and Reading & Writing Poetry at Griffith University, Gold Coast, and lives at Casuarina, on the far north coast of New South Wales.

Michelle Leber is a Melbourne poet. Her forthcoming book is a mythography in verse based on the Yellow Emperor of China (27th Century BCE), to be published by Five Islands Press in 2014.

Geoffrey Lehmann's *Poems 1957–2013* will be published by UWA Publishing in 2014. He co-edited (with Robert Gray) *Australian Poetry Since 1788*, published by UNSW Press, which was among the *Economist*'s best books of 2011.

Bella Li is a Melbourne editor and PhD candidate, and a managing co-editor at Five Islands Press. Her poems have been published in *Meanjin, Cordite, Otoliths, Mascara Literary Review, Peril Magazine, Rabbit, The Best Australian Poems 2012* (Black Inc., 2012) and *Contemporary Asian Australian Poets* (Puncher & Wattmann, 2013). Her chapbook *Maps, Cargo* is forthcoming from Vagabond Press.

Rosanna Licari's poetry collection *An Absence of Saints* won the 2009 Thomas Shapcott Poetry Prize, the 2010 Anne Elder Award and was shortlisted for the 2010/2011 Mary Gilmore Award. Her poems won the 2011 Wesley Michel Wright Prize. In June 2013 she was a fellow at Hawthornden International Retreat in Scotland.

Kate Lilley has published two books of poetry, *Versary* (Salt, 2002) and *Ladylike* (UWAP, 2012), and the Vagabond Press chapbooks *Round Vienna* (2011) and *Realia* (2013). She is an associate professor in the English Department at the University of Sydney.

Debbie Lim was born in Sydney. Her awards include the Rosemary Dobson Prize (2009). A chapbook, *Beastly Eye*, was published by Vagabond Press in 2012. She is currently working on her first full-length collection.

Cameron Lowe's poetry collections are the chapbook *Throwing Stones at the Sun* (2005) and *Porch Music* (2010), both published by Whitmore Press; a third collection, *Circle Work*, is forthcoming from Puncher & Wattmann. He is currently completing a PhD at the University of Melbourne. He lives in Geelong.

Kent MacCarter is a writer and editor in Melbourne. He's the author of two poetry collections – *In the Hungry Middle of Here* (Transit Lounge, 2009) and *Ribosome Spreadsheet* (Picaro, 2011) – with a third, *Sputnik's Cousin*, coming out in 2014. MacCarter is active in Melbourne PEN. He is managing editor of *Cordite Poetry Review*.

Paul Magee is the author of *Cube Root of Book* (John Leonard Press, 2006); his second book of poetry is forthcoming from John Leonard Press. He also wrote the surreal ethnography *From Here to Tierra del Fuego* (University of Illinois Press, 2000). Paul studied in Melbourne, Moscow, San Salvador and Sydney, and teaches poetry at the University of Canberra.

Mark Mahemoff has been writing poetry since the mid-1980s. In 2000 he completed an MA in writing at the University of Technology, Sydney. He has published three books of poetry, the most recent being *Traps and Sanctuaries* (Puncher & Wattmann, 2008). He also plays drums and percussion in a variety of musical projects.

Jennifer Maiden has published seventeen poetry collections and two novels. She has received many awards, including the *Age* Poetry Book of the Year (twice), the overall *Age* Book of the Year, the C. J. Dennis and the Christopher Brennan. She is the only writer to have been awarded the Kenneth Slessor three times. Her latest collection, *Liquid Nitrogen*, was published by Giramondo in 2012.

Caitlin Maling has published poetry, non-fiction and criticism throughout Australia and the United States. Her first collection, *Conversations I've Never Had*, is forthcoming in 2015 from Fremantle Press. Originally from Western Australia, she is currently based in Houston, Texas.

David Malouf is a poet and author of many books, including *An Imaginary Life, Harland's Half Acre, The Conversations at Curlow Creek, The Great World, Remembering Babylon, Typewriter Music* and *Ransom*. He lives in Sydney.

David McCooey is a prize-winning poet and critic. He is Personal Chair at Deakin University in Geelong, where he lives.

Mal McKimmie's first volume of poetry, *Poetileptic*, was published in 2005 by Five Islands Press. His second full collection, *The Brokenness Sonnets I–III & Other Poems*, also published by Five Islands Press, won the 2012 *Age* Poetry Book of the Year.

Ainslee Meredith is a poet and cultural conservation student from Melbourne. Her poems have appeared in several print and online literary journals, and she is a past recipient of the John Marsden Prize for Young Australian Writers. Her first collection, *Pinetorch*, was published in 2013 by Express Media/Australian Poetry.

Kate Middleton is a poet and essayist. Her first collection of verse, *Fire Season* (Giramondo, 2009), won the WA Premier's Award for Poetry and was shortlisted for the *Age* Poetry Book of the Year. Her latest book is *Ephemeral Waters* (Giramondo, 2013).

Peter Minter is a leading Australian poet, editor and poetry scholar. He is poetry editor of *Overland* and a senior lecturer in English at the University of Sydney, where he works in environmental poetics.

Paul Mitchell has published two poetry collections, *Minorphysics* (IP, 2003) and *Awake Despite the Hour* (Five Islands Press, 2007). He was a judge of the 2013 Victorian Premier's Literary Award for Poetry. www.paul-mitchell.com.au.

Les Murray's work has been published in many languages. He has won numerous literary awards, including the T. S. Eliot Award (1996) and the 1999 Queen's Gold Medal for Poetry, on the recommendation of Ted Hughes.

David Musgrave is the publisher at Puncher & Wattmann. He is a poet and novelist and teaches creative writing at the University of Newcastle.

Nguyen Tien Hoang is a Melbourne poet and translator. He is on the editorial panel of literary e-magazine *damau.org*. His most recent publication is *Years, Elegy* (Vagabond Press, 2012).

Jal Nicholl lives in Melbourne, where he writes and paints as much as his time and work commitments allow.

Ella O'Keefe lives in Melbourne. She is a doctoral candidate at Deakin University and is writing on the poetry of Barbara Guest and Veronica Forrest-Thomson. Her radio work has been broadcast on 2SER FM, FBI Radio and Radio National. Her poems have been published in *Cordite*, *Steamer* and the electronic collection *Mud Map: Australian Women's Experimental Writing*.

Louise Oxley has published two collections, *Compound Eye* (2003) and *Buoyancy* (2008). *Buoyancy* was shortlisted in the 2008 WA Premier's Literary Awards. In 2011 she was writer-in-residence at the University of Prince Edward Island, Canada. She spends as much time as she can in the peaceful D'Entrecasteaux Channel, south of Hobart, which is the setting for 'The Bat Corridor'.

Geoff Page is a Canberra-based poet. His most recent books are *Cloudy Nouns* (Picaro Press, 2012) and *1953* (UQP, 2013). His new books *Improving the News* (Pitt Street Poetry) and *New Selected Poems* (Puncher & Wattmann) are forthcoming.

π.O. was raised in inner-city Melbourne. Occupation: draughts-man. Disposition and history: anarchist. His collection of poems is *Big Numbers* (Collective Effort Press, 2008). He has represented Australia at many international festivals and is editor of the experimental magazine *Unusual Work*.

Felicity Plunkett's *Vanishing Point* (UQP, 2009) won the Arts Queensland Thomas Shapcott Prize and was shortlisted for the WA Premier's Book Awards, the Anne Elder Award and the Judith Wright Prize. *Seastrands* was published in Vagabond Press's Rare Object Series. She is the editor of *Thirty Australian Poets* (UQP, 2011).

Born in Brisbane in 1929, **Peter Porter** lived most of his life in England. He received, among other awards, the Forward Poetry Prize, the Queen's Gold Medal for Poetry, the Philip Hodgins Memorial Medal and the *Age* Book of the Year. Peter Porter died on 23 April 2010. This poem is published with the permission of his estate.

Claire Potter was born in Perth, WA. She has published three poetry collections, *Swallow* (Five Islands Press), *N'ombre* (Vagabond Press) and *In front of a comma* (Poets Union). She lives in London.

Judith Rodriguez has been publishing poems since the 1960s. Her latest are in the chapbook *The Manatee* (Picaro Press, 2007) and *The Hanging of Minnie Thwaites* (Arcade Books, 2012), and she edited *The Soliloquist* (Melbourne Shakespeare Society, 2013). She lives in Melbourne and works for International PEN.

Aden Rolfe is a writer and editor whose practice includes poetry, radio and criticism. His poems have been published in the *Age*, *Best Australian Poems 2011* and *Cordite Poetry Review*. He was featured in *Overland*'s Emerging Poets Series, and he is the 2013 recipient of the Dorothy Hewett Flagship Fellowship for Poetry.

Peter Rose is the author of the award-winning family memoir *Rose Boys* (2001), just reissued as a Text Classic. He has also published five poetry collections, most recently *Crimson Crop* (UWA Publishing, 2012), which won a 2012 Queensland Literary Award. He is the editor of *Australian Book Review*.

Josephine Rowe is the author of the short-story collections *How a Moth Becomes a Boat* (Hunter Publishers, 2010) and *Tarcutta Wake*

(UQP, 2012), which was longlisted for the 2013 Frank O'Connor International Short Story Award. She currently lives in Montreal.

Robyn Rowland has written nine books, including six of poetry. *Seasons of doubt & burning: New & selected poems* (2010) represents forty years of work. *Silence & its tongues* (2006) was shortlisted for the 2007 ACT Judith Wright Poetry Prize. In 2010 she won the Writing Spirit Poetry Award, Ireland.

Brendan Ryan grew up on a dairy farm at Panmure, in western Victoria. His second collection of poetry, *A Paddock in his Head* (Five Islands Press, 2007), was shortlisted for the 2008 ACT Poetry Prize. His most recent collection is *Travelling Through the Family* (Hunter Publishers, 2012). He lives in Geelong, where he teaches English at a secondary college.

Gig Ryan's *New and Selected Poems* (Giramondo, 2011; also published in the UK as *Selected Poems*, Bloodaxe Books, 2012) was winner of the 2012 Grace Leven Prize for Poetry and the 2012 Kenneth Slessor Prize for Poetry. She is poetry editor of the *Age* and a freelance reviewer.

Tracy Ryan is a West Australian writer who has also lived in the UK and the USA. She has published seven volumes of poetry, most recently *Unearthed* (Fremantle Press, 2013). She has also published three novels; a fourth, *Claustrophobia*, is due to appear in 2014 with Transit Lounge.

Andrew Sant's most recent collections of poetry are *Tremors: New and Selected Poems* (Black Pepper, 2004), *Speed & Other Liberties* (Salt Publishing, 2008), *Fuel* (Black Pepper, 2009) and *The Bicycle Thief & Other Poems* (Black Pepper, 2013). He lives in Melbourne.

Brenda Saunders has published three collections of poetry, and her work has appeared in selected anthologies and journals. She is a member of DiVerse poets, a group who write and read their ekphrastic poetry at various Sydney art galleries. Brenda recently returned from a Resident Fellowship at CAMAC Arts Centre in France, where she worked on translations of her poetry into French.

Jaya Savige is the author of *Latecomers* (UQP, 2005), which won the NSW Premier's Kenneth Slessor Prize for Poetry, and *Surface to Air* (UQP, 2011). He is a Gates Scholar at the University of Cambridge,

Christ's College, and Lecturer in English at A. C. Grayling's New College of the Humanities in Bloomsbury, London. As well as family and friends, he misses Milo, surfing in boardshorts and geckos.

Mandy Sayer is a novelist, memoirist and short story writer. She has written poetry since the age of six but only began submitting her work for publication in 2011. Her poems have since appeared in the *Australian Literary Review* and the *Australian.*

Oscar Schwartz is currently writing a PhD in philosophy, addressing the question of whether computers are able to write poetry. His work is published online and can be viewed at www.scarschwartz.com.

Thomas Shapcott was born in 1935 and has had many poems published. His latest book, *Parts of Us*, was published by UQP in 2010. He is still writing.

Laura Jan Shore is the author of *Breathworks* (Dangerously Poetic Press) and *Water over Stone* (Interactive Press), winner of IP Picks Best Poetry 2011. She won the 2012 Martha Richardson Poetry Prize, the 2009 F. A. W. John Shaw Nielson Award and the 2006 C. J. Dennis Open Poetry Award, and her poetry's been internationally published.

Vivian Smith's most recent book is *Here, There and Elsewhere* (Giramondo, 2012). He also co-edited *Windchimes: Asia in Australian Poetry* (Pandanus Press, 2006).

James Stuart's first full-length collection of poems, *Anonymous Folk Songs*, is forthcoming from Vagabond Press. His other book is *Imitation Era* (Vagabond Press, 2012). He was a 2008 Asialink literature resident in Chengdu, China, and works as a communications manager.

Maria Takolander is the author of two books of poems, *Ghostly Subjects* (Salt, 2009) and *The End of the World* (Giramondo, forthcoming), and a book of short stories, *The Double* (Text, 2012). She is a senior lecturer in literary studies and professional and creative writing at Deakin University in Geelong, Victoria.

Richard Kelly Tipping currently lives in Sydney, writing a book of anecdotes and working with visual poetry and public sculpture. The National Gallery of Australia, Canberra, lists and illustrates more than 100 of his word works through www.artsearch.nga.gov.au. A fat book of his concrete and spoken poems is nearing completion for Puncher & Wattmann in 2014.

John Tranter has published more than twenty collections of verse. His collection *Urban Myths: 210 Poems: New and Selected* won a number of major prizes. His latest book is *Starlight: 150 Poems* (UQP, 2010). He is the founding editor of the free internet magazine *Jacket*, and he has a homepage and journal at www.johntranter.net.

Ann Vickery is a senior lecturer in literary studies at Deakin University. She is the author of *Leaving Lines of Gender* (2000) and *Stressing the Modern* (2007), and co-author (with Maryanne Dever and Sally Newman) of *The Intimate Archive* (2009). She recently guest-edited 'The Political Imagination' issue of *Southerly* with Ali Alizadeh, and edited the 'Masque' issue of *Cordite Poetry Review*.

Corey Wakeling is the author of *Goad Omen* (Giramondo, 2013). With Jeremy Balius, Corey co-edited *Outcrop: radical Australian poetry of land* (Black Rider Press, 2013). He is reviews editor of poetry journal *Rabbit*, and interviews editor of *Cordite*.

Chris Wallace-Crabbe was born in 1934. His first collection of poetry was published in Australia in 1959. He has taught at the universities of Yale, Harvard and Venice, and is now professor emeritus in the Australian Centre at Melbourne University. Carcanet has published his *New and Selected Poems* (2013) and seven previous collections.

Alan Wearne continues assembling his verse narratives with forays into sonnets, villanelles and ballades. His friend, exemplary poet John Forbes, died the day the gangster Alphonse Gangitano was buried; their careers form strands in Alan's sequence 'The Vanity of Australian Wishes', which is, in part, his elegy for John.

Gemma White lives in Melbourne. She is a painter, poet, editor and founder of Only Words Apart Media (www.owamedia.com). Her work has appeared in magazines, anthologies and journals, including the *Age* and *Award Winning Australian Writing 2011*. Her first book of poetry, *Furniture Is Disappearing*, is due for release next year with IP.

Petra White's books are *The Incoming Tide* (John Leonard Press, 2007) and *The Simplified World* (John Leonard Press, 2010), which won the Grace Leven Prize. She lives in Melbourne.

Jessica L. Wilkinson's first poetry book, *marionette: a biography of miss marion davies*, was published by Vagabond Press in 2012. Her second book, *Suite for Percy Grainger*, will be published by Vagabond in 2014. She is the editor-in-chief of *Rabbit: a journal for non-fiction poetry*.

R. D. (Robert) Wood is a writer who has had work published in Australia, the United Kingdom, India and the United States. He is currently working on an uncreative chapbook.

Fiona Wright is a doctoral candidate with the University of Western Sydney Writing & Society Research Centre. Her poetry collection *Knuckled* (2011) won the Dame Mary Gilmore Award for a first collection in 2012.

Ouyang Yu came to Australia at the age of thirty-five. Now fifty-eight, he has published seventy-one books in English and Chinese languages, including his collection of English poetry *The Kingsbury Tales: A Complete Collection* (2012), his collection of English-Chinese bilingual poetry *Self Translation* (2012), and his translation into Chinese of *The Fatal Shore* (forthcoming in 2014).